From Protest to Resistance

Lilli Segal

English Edition

First published by Dog Ear Publishing
4010 W. 86th Street, Ste H
Indianapolis, IN 46268
www.dogearpublishing.net

ISBN: 978-1-4575-1040-3

This book is printed on acid-free paper.

Printed in the United States of America

REVIEWS:

The English translation of this memoir is a welcome and valuable addition to both Holocaust and World Literature. A rare and insightful look at the tumultuous period following World War I as seen through the eyes if a young woman growing up in pre-Nazi Germany. Lilli Segal's memoir takes us through the early years of World War II, including the fall of France, her subsequent capture by the Gestapo and, eventually, a thrilling escape from a labor camp of Auschwitz. Beautifully written.

Dr. Newman Fisher, *Professor Emeritus of Mathematics and Associate Dean - San Francisco State University*

Lilli's life is interpenetrated by the struggle between two "isms" that characterize the first half of the 20th century's footprint in history. As a university student active in the Communist party in post-World War I Germany, Lilli recognized fascism as a deadly dystrophic delusion earlier than most in the Western World. While millions paid with their lives for this mistake, Lilli survived concentration camps, prisons, and a stunning series of hairs-breadth escapes. She and her husband from college days developed brilliant scientific careers after World War II in East Germany, having never abandoned their original faith in the Marxist solution. This personal account illuminates the underlying political and economic forces that split European society between the two World Wars, and drove the conflict in the in the 2nd half of the century.

Michael Thaler, MD, *Professor of Medecine and Lecturer in History. University of California, Berkeley*

TABLE OF CONTENTS

Preface vii

Acknowledgments ix

I.   Childhood
      1918 – 1923 1-20

II.   Family – Death of Mother
      1923 – 1928 21-32

III. Education – Secondary School in Berlin
      1928 – 1933 33-53

IV.   Death of Father – Life in Paris
      1933...54-59

V.   University of Toulouse – Jascha
      1934 – 1937 60-74

VI.   Protest
      1937 – 1939 75-91

VII. Tour de France
      1940...92-104

VIII. Resistance – André
      1940 – 1943 105-129

IX.   Arrest in France
      1943 – 1944 130-146

X.   German Military Prison – Fresnes
        1943 147-177

XI.   Life in Auschwitz – Anni
        1944 178-206

XII.   Escape from Auschwitz
        1944 207-214

XIII.   Flight to Freedom
        1944 215-229

XIV.   Return to Life – Michael
        1945 – 1975 230-234

XV.   Post Script to New Edition
        1991 235-236

XVI   After the War 237-238

XVII   Maps 239

Preface

My Aunt Lilli, always rebellious and energetic, led an adventurous life. She studied in Germany, Switzerland and France, while actively participating in politics. During World War II she fled from the German troops on bicycle across France, was active in the French resistance movement, was imprisoned both in France and Germany, and escaped from Auschwitz, traversing war-torn Germany to Switzerland.

After the war she returned to Paris and rejoined her husband Jascha, who had given up all hope of a reunion. They were offered professorships at Humboldt University in East Berlin and decided to return to Germany to "assure that the Holocaust would not be repeated by the next generation." She became a well-known biochemist who went on extensive lecture tours and wrote numerous articles.

I was Lilli's "first child" and she was my second mother who carefully supervised my studies and activities after my recently widowed mother left me in her care on November 9th 1938, the eve of the historic Kristallnacht. I would stay with her for three years in France before rejoining my mother in New York. The bond between Lilli and me was very strong. Later, when I was an adult, I made many trips to France and Germany and eventually Lilli and Jascha visited my husband and me in California. Lilli especially enjoyed her jaunts to Mexico and Disneyland. We kept up a steady correspondence and remained in close contact until her death in 1999.

This memoir was published in Germany in 1986, followed by a second edition in 1991 entitled *Vom Widerspruch zum Widerstand*. All who have read it have encouraged me to have it translated into English, in the hope that Lilli will inspire new readers as much as she inspired all those who knew her.

Margo Kaufman

Acknowledgments

Lilli's niece Marga

When this memoir was first published in Germany in 1986 by my aunt, Lilli Segal, I wanted my family to read it, and I was further encouraged to publish the book in English by those who were familiar with Lilli's extraordinary life. The Holocaust Museum in San Francisco recommended John Bass, who provided an excellent translation and became the book's (and Lilli's) greatest admirer. His enthusiasm, advice, and support have been invaluable. I express my great appreciation to Dr. Ruth Lewin Sime, a published author, for her insights into the editing, and also to Dr. Newman Fisher, whose familiarity with the events of the time were of great help. I am grateful to Beth Mora for her help with the dreaded computer and her knowledge of the publication process. Finally, I thank Mark Jackson and Amber Ortner at Dog Ear Publishing, whose attention and care have made this book a reality.

by Margo "Marga" Kaufman

CHAPTER I

1918 – 1923

Childhood

"In contrast to my sister I had no feminine virtues whatsoever."

T he days of the revolution of November, 1918 are among the first impressions of my life. I was five and one half years old, my brother Herbert was nine and my sister Gerda was already eleven and one half. My mother was bedridden with a high fever; she was suffering from a dangerous erysipelas, because of this my father had been given 48 hours leave from the front line, which he spent at home with us in Berlin. We children had just recovered from the Spanish flu, but because the sickroom, which was the only heated room in our apartment, had to be kept quiet, we were put into overcoats and banished to the so called den. Its windows looked out on the street. The house stood at the corner of Martin Luther Strasse and Kleist Strasse which connected Wittenberg Platz with Nollendorf Platz and even then was one of the busiest streets in Berlin. Even on the fourth floor we could hear shouting and noise. Something strange was happening down there. The three of us flattened our noses against the windowpane to see what the groups of people on the street were up to. Several men in caps and armbands were haranguing a tall man in uniform and tearing something out of his grasp.

"They're taking his weapon away from him," my brother explained to me.

My sister was speechless with fright.

A car stopped on the opposite side of the street. Another group, which included a woman, opened the car door and, with an unmistakable gesture, they invited the officer sitting in the car to get out. He appeared to refuse. As they pulled him out, he raised his arm. At the same moment one of the men grabbed him and held him while another tore off his belt buckle and his shoulder straps. Then the people standing around stepped aside and politely made room for him to pass, accompanied by shouts and gestures. Another officer, who was sitting in a droshky, got less gentle treatment. He had tried to grab the reins out of the driver's hands and drive the carriage into the crowd. Yelling loudly, the crowd stripped him of his cap and overcoat. Then he too was allowed to run away. I thought all this activity was wonderful, for which my brother and sister scolded me.

Our noise disturbed Frieda, our housemaid of many years, and she came to see what was going on. The three of us made our reports to her and of course I tried to outdo the others.

"That's no big deal," said Frieda. "Those stuck up jerks are just getting what's coming to them."

My sister started to cry. "Well, what if they treat our Papa like that? He's an officer too!" "But he's not one of the ones that mistreats the troops," was Frieda's prompt answer. "He was telling us the soldiers at the front chose him to be one of their negotiators."

Frieda wasn't the only one, at that time, who sympathized with the revolutionaries and the strikers. After my mother's condition had improved and my father had come back to Berlin to stay,

Herbert, Gerda, and Lilli Schlesinger

there were constant political discussions in our home with relatives, with friends of my father and with some of the doctors who were working in his clinic. I remember my father, filled with rage, telling us how twelve of his fellow officers in Poland had slaughtered a pig and then eaten every bit of it, while the troops starved.

As soon as my father was demobilized he recommenced his work at his private clinic and at a polyclinic. In the afternoons and evenings he held consulting hours in our apartment. That created problems because, aside from the consulting room, only one room could be heated and we three children were romping around in it, even when my mother, who was seriously diabetic, needed a quiet hour. When the electricity was turned off all the oil lamps were moved into the consulting room and we sat in the dark. Although Frieda had to help out during consulting hours, my mother always managed to put a meal on the table punctually and even to entertain guests.

I greatly enjoyed this state of affairs. Up till then my brother and sister and I had, despite wartime conditions, led very sheltered lives, but now, when they were at school, there was no one to look after me. Barely six years old, I was allowed to make little purchases for myself and to play alone on the street. Later I was even permitted to go to the Zoological Garden by myself and wander around; when I did that I usually forgot to come home on time. We no longer had a nursemaid and my mother and the housemaids had their hands full keeping up with the most basic chores.

When a strike was called, the bathtub, the washtub and every other large container would be filled with water, but that wasn't nearly enough for the consulting room, so I was sent out to fetch water. At that time in Berlin there were still horse troughs into which water could be pumped up by hand. Long lines formed at these pumps. The Berliners waited patiently until they could fill their buckets and pots with the precious water. Standing in line at the pump was my favorite past-time. People told stories held disputes and cracked jokes and sometimes they said nice things about me because I was being good and helping my Mama. That was the right life for me and I felt very important. Unlike my brother and sister, I was not afraid, perhaps because I trusted my father so much and he trusted the people in the street.

Dr. Arthur Schlesinger, Lilli's Father with Dr. Bruno Wolff
in front of their clinic in 1922.

4

Lilli's father, Dr. Arthur Schlesinger

The polyclinic in which my father held consulting hours from eleven to one was housed in an apartment building at the corner of Hannover Strasse and Friedrich Strasse. My father took me there in the spring of 1920 to have me treated by an ear, nose and throat doctor. When we came out of the house and wanted to go to the subway we saw that a high barricade had been erected. Undeterred, my father went up to one of the men with an armband and said, " "I've got to go across here; can you take care of the little one for me?"

"Sure indeed!" was the reply. The man picked me up and another one took me and passed me on to an enormously fat man with a chubby face and merry blue eyes. In a deep bass voice he asked: "Now then, little Mam'sell, are you scared?"

"No!" I blurted out loud and clear, "Not a bit!"

"Well, you're right; nobody here is going to do anything to hurt our Doctor." And then he turned me over to my father, who in the meantime had climbed over a pile of stones, barrels, and boxes.

Later, at mealtime, my father told about our joint adventure. This time, though, my mother was rather concerned. "You really shouldn't take the children to Friedrich Strasse, when there's so much trouble," she said reproachfully, to which my father responded with a smile and a, "Well, yes... ."

Although June 7, 1919 was my sixth birthday, I still did not start school. My mother's long illnesses and her sanatorium cures were a burden on the household during this time and I was often sick myself. Someone or other taught me reading and writing at home. I had already learned to count and do simple arithmetic through the games I played with my older siblings, so that I could skip the first year of school. Reading immediately became my favorite occupation, while my attempts at writing, on the other hand, were so clumsy and my notebooks so blotchy that they earned me plenty of slaps from my seriously ill and temperamental mother.

To get me out of the way, the family would often ship me off to my grandparents in Dresden, or to a Protestant children's home in Kipsdorf, where I eagerly took part in the Sunday School and quickly learned all the hymns by heart. At that time I was not aware that I actually belonged to a Jewish family.

My grandfather, Siegfried Schlesinger, had come to Dresden in the mid-1870s, near the end of the economic boom that followed the Franco-Prussian war and the founding of the German Empire. A simple commercial employee, he brought with him his wife, the daughter of a well-to-do middle class family. He opened a store in Dresden, specializing in oriental carpets. At that time oriental carpets were still actually being made in the Orient, then sold in Germany after being traded through Bulgaria and Vienna. There was a whole chain of middlemen. My grandfather's idea was to travel to Constantinople and Sofia himself and buy the goods directly in the factories. The direct carpet sales and the founding of a large ready-made clothing store in the center of

Dresden made him into a wealthy man in the course of two decades.

Siegfried Schlesinger, German Counsel General to Persia (Iran)

My grandfather was a decided snob and he paid money to obtain the title of a General Consul of Persia. He expected people to use this title when speaking to him. He was admitted to the Royal Court of Saxony, where he looked very smart in his court uniform with its astrakhan lamb's wool trim. Since the courtiers did a lot of hunting, he leased a large estate bordering on a royal hunting preserve. In Grandfather's household Judaism played an even smaller role than it did with us in Berlin. His people wanted to belong to the society of the Saxon Royal Court.

One of our favorite games in Dresden was "find the keys". My grandparents' domestic staff had been with the family for years, beginning with Lenka, the old cook and the Lorenz couple who had grown old and grey in the family's service, down to the young, pretty Else, who took care of my grandmother, did her hair, accompanied her on journeys, took care of her wardrobe, sewed, ironed – a lady's maid, as the elegant term was then. The relationship to all these members of the household was a patriarchal one, although marked by mutual trust – which still did not keep my grandmother Rosamunde from locking up every pound of coffee, every tin of cookies and every crystal goblet. The wine cellar and the larder each had a different key and they all hung on one key ring or another.

Schlesinger home in Dresden

Since my grandmother's sight was very poor and various cupboards had to be locked constantly throughout the entire house, she was forever misplacing one of her key rings. We children were allowed to look for it. That was great fun, especially because it gave us the chance to disturb the salons and the library, which otherwise were forbidden to us.

During my stays in Dresden I was mostly entrusted to good-natured Lenka, but often as well to Mr. Lorenz, the factotum of the household. Each of them spoiled me, to which I responded with great

Lilli's mother, Fania

affection. The only person of whom I stood in awe was my grandfather, who was very ill and whom I seldom saw.

My thirst for adventure remained as strong as ever. Although I certainly enjoyed the big garden attached to the house, I still wanted company. So I would either sneak out the garden gate onto the street, or open the gate to let other children in from the street and play with them in the garden. The adults didn't stop me from doing this, but they did note with disapproval that I was assimilating all the strong language used by the street boys. They especially disap-proved that I always looked like a bandit – with cuts on my knees and bruises. I, of course, wanted to show the boys that I could climb just like they did. Lorenz wasn't always able to hide my escapades from Grandmother. She would clap her hands together above her head and give me a moral lecture. But because I had once chanced to overhear a conversation in which Grandmother was complaining to my mother about my upbringing and my mother was vehemently defending me and the street kids, the lec-tures remained unsuccessful.

Family vacation: Dr. Arthur Schlesinger, Fania and guests.

My mother made some other remarks which made it clear to me, as far as I was able to understand, that she despised elegant society and people who were conceited about their money. She herself, a poor girl from a provin-cial town in Romania, had been brought up by an aunt in Vienna. When she had completed her schooling she did not want to go on the marriage market, as the custom then was, and she managed to complete a course in dentistry. But without capital she wasn't able to set up her own practice and because she was a woman no one wanted to hire her. Everyone advised her to give up and go back to Romania. Proud as she was, she took a job as a nurse rather than give up. At the hospital she got to know my father, who was working as an assistant physician.

My mother was a beauty. With her black hair, big brown eyes and light complexion, full-bosomed but very slender of limb and narrow of waist, the fashions of those years suited her especially well. From among her different admirers my mother chose my father out of genuine love. My grandfather, who was otherwise such a snob, quickly warmed to his beautiful, original daughter-in-law while, even years after the wedding, various remarks of my grandmother made it clear that she did not regard the poor girl, in addition to everything else a Jewess from the East, as a socially suitable wife for her son. From conversations between my father and my mother I understood that we were Jews, although we celebrated Christmas and Easter like any normal Protestant family.

I still remember the big demonstration of the Berlin workers protesting against the murder of the Foreign Minister Walther Rathenau by anti-Semitic nationalistic officers. The demonstrators marched for hours down Kleist Strasse with red flags, singing. Impassionedly my mother declared to my father that he should have no illusions, hatred of Jews was thriving and it would avail German Jews and their families nothing, if those who were former officers proclaimed their loyalty to the Kaiser or tried to ingratiate themselves with the Nationalists.

Grandfather died in the summer of 1922. My father sold the luxury villa in Dresden and the estate. He discharged the staff and paid them compensation, so that in later years we kept up friendly relations. Grandmother moved in with us. The apartment in Kleist Strasse was too small and the decision was made to live in a villa again. Suedende (South End) was chosen, an unattractive suburb, without woods, without water, but with an excellent urban railway connection to Potsdamer Platz. From there my father could walk to his clinic in 10 minutes, which was located in Koeniggratz Strasse, later Stresemann Strasse.

My father owned a little electric car back then, a two-seater with a top speed of 35 kilometers per hour and a battery whose charge was adequate for about 50 kilometers. During the week he used it mainly to drive back and forth between his clinic and the polyclinic in Hannover Strasse; on Sundays he would drive it out to Suedende to properly recharge the battery. During the cold weather that wasn't enough. The battery would fail and colleagues and acquaintances told of meeting Dr. Schlesinger and his assistant in Friedrich Strasse or Leipziger Strasse, pushing the mini-car.

Despite her severe diabetes, my mother insisted on taking an active role in furnishing the villa in Suedende. At the beginning of December 1922, completely exhausted, she took to her bed with pneumonia and a high fever - her heart failed her. She died within three days.

I can barely remember the year following her death. For a while, a female cousin of my father from the Berlin branch of the family managed the household; then relatives of my mother came from Romania and tried to reorganize it, until my father finally engaged a housekeeper. This was Miss Mehne, who had lost her fiancé in the war. As the daughter of a postal employee, without independent means, she had to earn her living somehow. She was friendly, good-hearted, had a sound public school education and was completely apolitical and interested in the normal life of a German housewife. Since she had previously lived with the family of a Jewish artist in Berlin, I was able to learn one or two things about Judaism from her.

Whenever, in that big eight-person household, where people were always visiting, many of them staying overnight, my father decided to save on something he thought was too elegant or unnecessary, she never dared to oppose my him. She herself was always very cautious in regard to questions of cost. She was unable to restrain my brother who was already at fourteen and fifteen, involved in serious flirtations. The only one who accepted her guidance was my sister, who was obedient and neat. After completing her tenth year at school, my sister enrolled in a home economics school in a small provincial town.

My relationship to Miss Mehne was neutral. In contrast to my sister I had no feminine virtues whatsoever. I was not neat and had no feeling for appearances or good manners. My father treated me like a boy; he took me everywhere with him and tried to interest me in everything that he himself thought was fun. He talked seriously to me about everything – history, his travels, churches, museums, sporting events. I was his darling. My brother had inherited my grandfather's vein of liberality and soon began making fun of our father's parsimony and his simple, upright ways. He had an interest in and a gift for technological matters, an area in which my father failed. On the other hand, he refused, from a spirit of opposition, to read serious books or to visit museums, not to mention churches.

I was constantly hanging on my father's arm, hugging him, going everywhere with him and taking a serious interest in his hobbies. When I was thirteen, I took my first trip alone with him to Switzerland, where we went hiking with our knapsacks on our backs. I was of course very proud to be treated almost as a grownup and behaved like a precocious smarty. In reality I was naive and innocent, especially in regard to anything having to do with sex.

In the Protestant religion classes, which I attended at my father's wish, I always got top grades. In the Christmas pageant I played the leading role several times. But when my fellow pupils showed me some passage in the Bible about the morals of King David or Abraham, I never understood a thing. I simply didn't know what they were giggling about.

My teachers, of course, simply didn't believe that an impudent brat like me, who moreover was the daughter of a physician, could possibly be naive. On the occasion of the wedding of my favorite teacher, who taught girl's gym, I wrote a play and performed it with some of the other pupils. The play was a big success which caused our German teacher to read through the script in order to search, albeit in vain, for questionable erotic and political material. He was, in 1925, already a hardcore Nazi.

Discotheques were still unknown back then. At parties we often sang Alpine folk songs. We sang risqué verses, some of which we made up ourselves, to simple melodies. I had composed about thirty rhyming verses making fun of our school and of individual teachers. During a school excursion on a steamer, these verses were sung by some of the schoolgirls and a scandal ensued. In fact, it was a matter of a few harmless jokes. The most serious were the announcements that the Social Democratic chemistry teacher wore a red necktie and that the school director, our religion teacher, was proud of having found an unknown Bible. This wasn't taken seriously but another of the verses almost got me kicked out of school. One of our women teachers was a German Nationalist member of the provincial parliament. She was constantly organizing patriotic demonstrations on behalf of the poor ethnic Germans living outside Germany, on the Memel, or in threatened Upper Silesia. In her class she took every opportunity to assign readings from the war memoirs of German officers and generals. She often proclaimed at the top of her voice that every real German woman had to bear at least ten children. I should add, that most of our women teachers were unmarried old maids since, according to the law at that time, female civil servants and teachers were not allowed to marry. I really didn't mean anything bad when I wrote "Dr. Neumann unfortunately has no husband/and so she can't have ten children." When this verse was shown to my father, as evidence of my depravity, he replied laconically that he didn't understand the complaint: I had simply expressed a fact, although quite clumsily. I suppose that it was due to his naiveté that I got off with a reprimand from the faculty council.

We really didn't understand why, of all places, we had to move to lower-middle class, reactionary Suedende-Mariendorf. All of our relatives and acquaintances lived in the western part of Berlin or in Pankow and Niederschoenhausen. Low-ranking civil servants and white collar employees lived here in the southwest also very few workers. Only in Mariendorf was there a section of row houses where a few highly skilled craftsmen lived. People read the German Nationalist local paper, or at best the populist Stresemann-oriented Volkszeitung. Aside from my family, only two of the families of my classmates took the democratic Vossische Zeitung. Even when Hindenburg was elected in 1929, it was hard to spot the official black-red-gold flag of the Republic among all the black-white-red flags. Red flags were simply not to be seen in our area.

In spring 1923 my brother was enrolled in the classical high school in neighboring Steglitz. After a week he refused to go back. When his name, Herbert Schlesinger, was announced to the class, one of the pupils called out, "What's this, a Jew-boy?" The class immediately organized a boycott. Nobody would talk to him, nobody would hand him anything and every day at noon his belongings would disappear. The teachers, who were observing the behavior of the class very closely, did nothing to put a stop to the boycott. So my brother returned to the Mommsen classical high school in Berlin-West where the people were reactionary but at least not anti-Semitic.

At my girl's middle school, most of the teachers, both men and women, were German Nationalist or loyal to the Kaiser; some, however, supported the Republic. From time to time they would remind us that we lived in a country in which everyone could lay claim to equal rights. On August 21, at the ceremony celebrating the adoption of the constitution of the Republic, these democratic gentlemen and one lady, arrived wearing formal attire. Most of the teachers, however, showed up dressed in an ostentatiously shabby fashion.

I was, of course, a black sheep, but still the daughter of Dr. Schlesinger, a respected Berlin physician, so I could permit myself the occasional escapade. On the other hand, no mercy was shown to the truly well-behaved, hard-working daughter of a skilled worker, who had an exemption from school fees and never took part in any pranks.

Inge, the daughter of an official in the railway service, a tall, powerfully built girl with long blonde pigtails and grey, almost colorless eyes in an angular, not unattractive face, was in the habit of shoving and abusing me, the smallest and youngest girl in the class. She seemed particularly annoyed that I was the favorite pupil of our director, who taught the class in Protestant religion. "My father" declared Inge, "says that if Jews take part in religion class, then it's just because they're scared." One day in drawing class she drew a swastika on the blackboard right next to where I was standing. The drawing teacher was busy, but wouldn't have done anything anyway. I demanded several times, rather loudly, that Inge erase the swastika. She just laughed, mockingly. As soon as the bell rang I wanted to hurl myself at her but she ran down the stairs and out to the schoolyard as quickly as she could. I ran after her and, wild with rage, before the other girls could get to the yard, I had struck her, taller than me by half a head, in the face with my fist. I hit her lower lip and chin. The girl was so surprised that she lost her balance and fell down. Blind with fury, I hammered away at her. Meanwhile the other pupils arrived and pulled us apart. Two of my friends dragged me to the washroom, while Inge, sobbing and bleeding from her lip, complained to the school authorities. Of course the class teacher called me on the carpet and I got an oral reprimand. My father was informed by telephone about my brutality. But once again he defended me against the swastika artist. There was, he said, no other response to anti-Semitic provocations. His defense succeeded: the director gave a talk in which he condemned the scrawling of swastikas and from then on Inge and her friends left me alone.

In 1929 my father was still prepared to speak out for the Republic and democracy, but even then he found no support in the lower middle class milieu that surrounded us. During physical education classes we were usually divided into two groups for team sports-volley ball, soccer, handball and the like. The teams wore colored ribbons with their white gym blouses, so that they could be told apart. One of our physical education teachers, who was also a German Nationalist, selected black-white-red ribbons for my team; our mothers were supposed to sew them for us. There was, of course, no team with black-red-gold or red ribbons.

My father was incensed at this political manifestation. He decided to send a letter of protest to the director of the school and to the physical education teacher. In good faith, he believed that senior civil servants of the Republic would join in his protest and he turned first to one of the fathers, an official in the Ministry of Health. He did not even get an answer. Then he paid a personal visit to the father of my best girlfriend. Dr. Erich, a state's attorney and later judge of a superior provincial court, father of five children, was the model of a correct, cultivated and tolerant citizen. When my father admonished him that, as a highly placed member of the judiciary, he should at the very least defend the Republic, he replied that precisely because of his position within the judicial system he should not under any circumstances interfere in political matters. My father sent his protest letter anyway. The physical education teacher did in fact have to withdraw the black-white-red ribbons. She did this with a spiteful speech about the intellectuals, for example a doctor, who suspected some wicked political machination behind everything. The class laughed.

When I recall these events, I have the feeling that my father and the few honest democrats whom I knew were on the defensive, while the German Nationalists and the warmongers were constantly seizing the initiative. Much later a wise man said to me: "The Weimar Republic was like a beautiful woman who was just waiting to be raped."

The brother of my grandmother, Emanuel Mendel, had been a well known Berlin physician. Today a street in Pankow is named after him. The Mendels either had themselves baptized or married Christian women; they conformed to the "good" national tradition. The progressive members of the family voted for Stresemann and apparently for the Republic. But there was also Uncle Fritz Mendel, an elegant dandy, who lived on Monbijou Platz where he kept his own horses in the courtyard. Up to 1934 he drove through Berlin in his coach, drawn by two white horses. He was actually an optometrist, but because of his charm he was under contract to eight Berlin theaters as a house physician. He was given two free tickets for every performance, which he distributed among the doctors of the family, because a doctor always had to be present in the hall. But quite often he would spend an evening driving in his coach from one theater to another himself. In his consulting room there hung a portrait of the Kaiser, where I saw it as late as 1935.

Kurt Mendel, his brother, was a neurologist and the family poet. I loved reciting his happy, nice, harmless verses at family gatherings. His wife, on the other hand, was of the same caliber as my German Nationalist female teachers and boasted to everyone of the genuine Prussian upbringing her offspring had enjoyed. I got into a quarrel with her conceited son Rudolf Mendel which established my reputation as the black sheep of the family. We were spending the winter vacation in a little hotel. My tall, lanky, blonde cousin Rudi made a comment that there were too many intellectual Jews in our group. I really don't know why I reacted as harshly as I did. Perhaps my quick-witted and clever brother had already said something to incite me, but I said loudly, "Well, if your name is Mendel and you're as dumb as you are, then you do need to watch out!" That was the beginning of a family boycott against me. Later, Rudolf Mendel was to pay a bitter price for his attitude. In 1933/34 he was working in a little village in Franconia. Thanks to his Christian upbringing and his good looks he made friends with the pretty daughter of the village pastor and became engaged to her. His mother was, of course, proud of this engagement, which warmed her Christian, nationalistic heart – up until the day when The Stormer (Der Stuermer), the anti-Semitic paper published by Mr. Julius Streicher, printed a caricature and an article with the headline: "Jew Rudolf Mendel Seduces Innocent German Girl." All I know is that he had to leave the village by the quickest route. From then on out the family really understood that they, too, were among the outlawed.

One of the Mendel daughters, Lotte Gradenwitz, had inherited her parents' villa in the Berliner Strasse in Pankow. The atmosphere there was just as hospitable as with us and the younger generation in particular liked to gather there. I was still too small and also too much in disfavor with the family to go there often. The Kuczynski siblings, who were related to the Gradenwitzes, liked to go there. Although they were the same age as my brother and sister, they were never invited to our home. My father found the Kuczynski's too radically leftwing.

I can still recall exactly the many discussions during 1925/26 about reparations for the princes. Under pressure from the aristocrats, the old officers and the haute bourgeoisie and above all from the German Nationalist President Hindenburg, the State of Prussia wanted to compensate the Hohenzollern family for all of the assets confiscated in November 1918. Further, they wanted to pay the former Kaiser, in addition to his annual pension of six hundred thousand marks, another one hundred and eighty-five million gold marks as reparations. The Communists and also the Social Democrats and some middle-class democrats as well, protested against this waste in a country that had provided no support whatever for the victims of war. Disabled veterans could be seen everywhere in Berlin: blind, missing both legs, mentally ill, they sat on the sidewalks trying to earn a few pennies by selling matches, shoe laces and postcards. The leftwing parties called for a referendum under the slogan "Not One Penny For The Princes." Robert Kuczynski had worked out a plan calling for the rejection of reparations payments by a plebiscite.

This plebiscite was discussed at school and in every family. It was precisely the lower-middle class residents of Mariendorf who defended the rights of the princes to reparations, even more strongly than the upper-middle class circles in which my father moved. With the help of a well thought out rightwing political campaign the princes recovered every penny. The initiatives of the workers' parties failed. They were portrayed as attacks on the principle of property as such, which would be followed by other attacks. In the opinion of my father many people would have been against total reparations, but Kuczynski and his radical friends had overplayed their hand. According to their plan the princes would have gotten nothing and many people thought that was unjust and immoderate.

My grandfather's family, the Schlesingers, were mainly businessmen. They were moderately conservative and not so nationalistic as the physicians; still, their contacts to my father's family were not very close. People came together at official family gatherings but they never discussed politics or ideologies on such occasions.

The younger people, many of whom also spent time at our home, were less reactionary.

In 1926 my nineteen year old sister became engaged to a doctor ten years her senior. My father insisted that she pass her nurse's examination before she got married. My father believed, unlike many of his friends and colleagues, that a married woman should have an occupation. One never knew what might happen and he did not want his daughters to suffer the fate of so many officers' widows, who had to eke out an existence as housekeepers, or as paid companions, or by subletting rooms in their dwellings. Fritz Freudenthal, the son of a Jewish country doctor, had volunteered for service in the war and had been at Verdun and many other battles in France and in 1918 had come home from the front with a wound and a kidney ailment. Fritz was a good natured, jolly, rather earthy Bavarian and was seriously in love with my sister, even though, once they were married, he indulged in all sorts of escapades. My sister, a good housewife, took hospitality for granted. My brother-in-law quickly became a popular doctor in Steglitz and the two of them kept an open, generous household.

Their friends were all of my brother-in law's generation. For most of them the war had been a sad experience that had devoured a part of their youth. In contrast to my father's generation, these young doctors and lawyers did not talk about their war experiences, but tried to throw themselves into the life of the postwar world and the wide variety of entertainments available in those years. They went out a lot. (My father found it almost immoral to go to a restaurant in Berlin.) My brother-in-law and my sister went to nightclubs and cabarets. The theater productions of Erwin Piscator and the operas of Bert Brecht and Kurt Weil were cultural events. Films like "The Blue Angel", "The Cruiser Potemkin" and "Storm Over Asia" aroused attention and people were enthused over Remarque's "All Quiet On The Western Front". When the Steel Helmets (Der Stahlhelm) a reactionary organization of former frontline soldiers and the first National Socialist groups, took open action against this, "treasonous, Bolshevik, pacifistic art" and physically attacked the audience in the cinemas, throwing stink bombs and shouting in chorus, people were indignant. A few courageous ones kept on going to the shows, but no one thought of putting up any serious opposition to the disturbances. While the right-wingers demanded, vociferously and forcibly, that measures must be taken to put a stop to this "intolerable cultural Bolshevism" only a handful of democratic citizens responded in any active way. Most just shrugged their shoulders or quoted Kurt Tucholsky, or Erich Kaestner, or in a few cases Erich Weinert, who was too radical for most of them.

Someone once said about Tucholsky that he was "to the left of himself". And that was true of the whole democratic left in those years: it was simply "to the left of itself."

Gerda, Herbert, Lilli

CHAPTER II

1923 – 1928

Family – Death of Mother

"From her different admirers my mother chose my father out of genuine love."

Immediately after my mother's death in 1923, female cousins came to Berlin from Romania for a long stay to manage the household and look after us children, mainly I believe, in the hope that my father would marry one of them. For women living in not very well-to-do circumstances in a small town in Romania, Vienna, Berlin and, of course, Paris represented the great, desirable world. But my father had no feeling for the elegance and femininity of our Romanian guests. One way or another he got rid of the ladies after some months. When, later on, they arrived for visits of two or three weeks, he was pleased to see them. Although conditions in Romania were semi-feudal and later became Fascistic, indeed perhaps it was precisely for that reason, my Romanian family was much more progressive than my German family. They were filled with a longing for democracy, for modern culture and even the younger girls, who had been raised by pious nuns, looked toward France, the land of the French Revolution, of the Paris Commune, the land of Jean Jaures and Briand.

My father was quite open to these influences. He liked to hear about the big, progressive world and he understood why the

Poles and the Balkan people regarded German imperialism as their enemy and looked to France as an ally in war and a friend. He was especially fond of a cousin of my mother, whom my mother had always treated like a brother. Uncle Max Zoller was actually a businessman with legal training. Because of his knowledge and intelligence the Romanians had made him a member of the commission which negotiated with Germany about reparations for war damages. He spent several months of each year in Berlin and my father always insisted that he stay with us. I remember him as a dainty little man with sharply defined facial features, a high forehead and white hair. All the ladies liked him and I believe that he had a series of love affairs. I idolized him. During discussions at the dinner table he was able to express his opinions in such refined German that my shy, by no means eloquent father usually yielded the point. He was never insulted when this happened; after a lengthy discussion he ungrudgingly recognized my uncle's superiority. Max Zoller had the standpoint of a Marxist theorist and his attitude was that of a left Social Democrat. He represented the standpoint that, although it might be unpleasant for "people like us", the capitalist system had run its course and communism was the only possible solution. He was a fanatical Francophile and thought that France had found a form of democracy that permitted that country to combine cultural continuity with social progress.

When I got a little older, he began to give me books by authors who were unknown even in our educated household – Romain Rolland, Anatole France, Barbusse, Zola, the Communist Manifesto, *"The Eighteenth Brumaire Of Louis Napoleon"* by Marx, the letters of Rosa Luxemburg and of August Bebel. To be sure, my father, my siblings, my brother in law and some of our acquaintances rejected Prussian-German chauvinism and militarism, but they really had nothing to oppose it with. But now I had found something that attracted me: a different, independent way of thinking, something that simple, timid rejection had not been able to accomplish.

My father, who had no understanding for anything connected with erotic matters, or with sexuality, was criticized by my grandmother and our housekeeper, for giving me books that, allegedly, dealt with sexual problems in an explicit manner. For example, when I was twelve and was sick in bed, he lent me Thomas Mann's *"Royal Highness"*. When the ladies of the house complained, he came to my bed and said, blushing, "I believe I'm going to have to take the book back; you're not ready for it yet."

"Oh" I answered, "if you mean the description of the birth and the congenital deformity at the beginning of the story, I've already read that. After all, I am a doctor's daughter and I do know what a difficult delivery is."

"Oh all right then, you can finish reading it," he said, relieved.

This sort of naiveté and, in a certain sense, asexuality seems to have been rather widespread among intellectual Jews of my father's generation. The postwar generation had a joke: "Why is making out with a Christian girl better than making out with a Jewish girl?" Answer: "The Christian girl yells out 'Jesus and Mary!' and Jesus and Mary never show up; the Jewish girl yells out 'Papa!' or 'Mama!' and Papa and Mama come running!" If the doctors of the postwar generation told an off-color joke at the dinner table, then my father would usually look around him with astonishment and ask my brother "Can you explain that to me?" His friends did the same. For my father and his friends there was no double morality. When my brother, as a student, was living together with a female student, my father urged him to marry: "You've compromised that girl! If it were my daughter I'd insist that the young man marry her."

In 1935 my brother was working as an assistant physician at the Jewish hospital in Berlin. Although he was only twenty-six years old he was often asked, in psychologically delicate situations, to talk to the husbands of female patients, "because Dr. Schlesinger doesn't have complexes like the Chief." In the same year my brother admitted me to the hospital because of an abdominal complaint. An operation appeared necessary. When he reported this to his boss, the surgeon, he was told: "Oh, your sister isn't married, bring her to our ward, that must be a complicated appendicitis." But when he scheduled me with the gynecologist Dr. Joseph and informed him that an abdominal operation would probably be necessary, he was quite astonished and asked, "Oh, is she married?"

My brother would tell this story to his friends and always end with the question, "Now I ask you, do I look like somebody who has a sister who is twenty-one years old and still hasn't found someone to deflower her?"

My brother got his driver's license when he was just seventeen. Because he suffered from a serious kidney complaint he wasn't able to play sports very much, so he made fun of my father's athletic enthusiasm. My father, on the other hand, had little sympathy for my brother's highly developed relationship to the opposite sex. He didn't talk about it directly, but made it clear that he disapproved of my brother's attitude.

Herbert really was a good looking boy. Dark-haired, with big brown eyes. very regular features, a good figure and winning smile. Intelligent and witty, vain and always well dressed, he was very interested in girls. We always wondered why my father always wore old neckties until we learned that my brother was wearing my father's new ties and hanging his old ones in my father's wardrobe.

We squabbled a lot, but I admired him nevertheless and was proud of the fact that a series of girls, one or two years older than I was, "hung out" with me because they wanted, by this means, to entice my brother. Despite the tender love that I felt for my father, I covered up my brother's flirtations, arranged rendezvous for him and took part in secret excursions, for which he would

24

misappropriate the paternal car from the garage and then pack it full of "young girls".

In a class parallel to mine there was a girl, barely sixteen, who often went swimming, bicycling and ice skating with me and was quite open about the fact that she was after my brother. Hilde Scheller was pretty. A regular, open face with big grey eyes. Very well developed. She was intelligent but a very poor student and took a leading part in all the school pranks. She often came to our home. I never went to hers. She described her parents as rigidly reactionary and opposed to having any visitors. It's possible, too, that her father forbade her having anything to do with Jews. The father believed that he could control Hilde and her brother Guenther through strict Prussian discipline. She frequently came to the swimming pool with blue and brown marks on her body. Her father beat her with a stick at every opportunity.

The crisis in our relationship began one evening when my father came home unexpectedly after nine o'clock and found Hilde Scheller with my brother on the sofa in the den. They were kissing each other so passionately that they did not hear my father when, not at all cautiously, he opened the door. Tempest in a teapot! Hilde Scheller was chased from the house under a hail of abjurations, forbidden ever to darken our door again. I was interrogated and insisted that my brother had brought Hilde home at nine o'clock, upon which I was grounded for an extended period.

Of course I saw Hilde at school and sometimes when swimming, but my brother tried very soon to discourage me from being too friendly with her. "Believe me, she's really not the right company for you," he said. And I soon saw myself that she had too many boys around her.

And then, in the summer of 1927, the drama unfolded. All the newspapers were full of it. Suddenly, at the kiosk in the Suedende train station, no newspapers were to be found. All the girls in the upper classes at school pounced on the daily press, especially if the papers had been hidden from them at home. What had happened? The Scheller parents had gone on a trip. Hilde used the opportunity to take a boyfriend, a seventeen year old apprentice cook, into the home and the bedroom of her parents. Her brother Guenther, a conceited, stupid senior, was sitting in the kitchen with Paul Krantz, a classmate of the same age, who probably was also in love with Hilde. At about nine in the evening my brother whistled in front of the house. Hilde came down and invited him to come in. The coast was clear. Guenther and Paul Krantz, who were already drunk, were looking out the window and also told him to come on up. However my brother wasn't in the mood and he quickly took his leave of Hilde. About half an hour later Guenther knocked on the bedroom door and demanded, beside himself with rage, that Hilde open up. No one ever learned exactly what happened next. Apparently Guenther pulled his sister's boyfriend from behind the curtain where he was hiding, fired one or two lethal shots with a revolver and went back to the kitchen. There he fired a bullet through his own head. The doctor who was called, an acquaintance of my father, was able only to ascertain that he was dead. As he told it, Krantz simply stood by, indifferent and let it all happen. Which, in the opinion of the doctor, stigmatized him at once as a sociopath. In addition, Krantz came from very poor circumstances, which prejudiced everyone against him both at school and in the suburb of Suedende.

The Scheller parents, when they returned to Berlin, instead of letting the matter rest, announced that they were determined to save the honor of their son and brought a complaint against Krantz for murder, naming as witnesses Hilde Scheller and her girlfriend Eleanor, a girl who had been expelled from the school because of some incident or other. In fact Krantz was arrested on the basis of this complaint and was held in investigative detention for more than a year, awaiting trial.

The Scheller trial made headlines for weeks in the Berlin papers. The issues that got the most attention were the credibility and morals of Hilde Scheller and the psychology and behavior of Paul Krantz. It was the topic of the day; people talked about it everywhere. I don't recall anyone asking why these young people had access to a revolver at all and what steps Mr. Scheller had taken to ensure that his son could not get hold of a weapon. The press showed no mercy whatsoever to Krantz, despite his youth, and publicized every little detail of his life. In regard to my brother, things were handled very differently. Because Herbert had been the last person to speak to both Hilde and Guenther Scheller on that tragic evening, he was summoned as a witness during the trial. Because of his kidney condition, it was easy to find a colleague of my father who certified that he was not able to be examined and cross-examined in court. To be sure, the papers printed my brother's statement, but only referred to him as Herbert S., without giving his name, his address, or the name of the school. I don't believe that my father bribed anyone, but I assume that patients of my father, somewhere within the legal system, perhaps in the public relations office, wanted to spare him.

I didn't know Krantz, but I was happy when he was finally acquitted. Because of this trial I started reading and thinking about the German legal system.

Lilli's step-mother Edith

At some point during the winter of 1927/28 my father informed me that he was going to marry again: Miss Edith Albrecht, the surgical nurse in his clinic, who had been a frequent guest in our home. Edith Albrecht was then twenty-six years old: small, slender, golden blonde (to be sure with a bit of chemical enhancement); she had blue eyes, a very elongated face, which made a rather severe impression and a dazzling figure. Her manner was decidedly feminine. She enjoyed flirting with young people and she understood how to deploy feminine weakness as a weapon. My father was like a new man.

For her sake, my father, who was then fifty-four, gave up mountain climbing, swimming and hiking. Instead of marching through museums and churches with a knapsack on his back and a Baedecker in his hand, he now settled in with his new wife at well-known spas or on an elegant beach. In the mornings the gracious lady, upon awakening, would ring and my father, who had already been up for a couple of hours, writing in his room, would then come to take breakfast at her bed.

Edith came from an impoverished officer's family; her parents were dead. She had studied nursing with a Lutheran nursing order, but left the order before coming to my father's clinic. Her younger brother, Jens Albrecht, who had attended cadet school, was an unemployed auto salesman. He soon became a constant guest, not only in our home, but at my sister's home at well. A nice, uncomplicated man, he behaved toward me as to a younger sister to whom one has to explain the facts of life. He found my total ignorance of money matters especially amusing.

Ruth, the beautiful and egotistical sister of Edith and Jens Albrecht, behaved in a completely different way. She was married to a lawyer who not only had the unpleasant, coarse face of a former member of a student dueling fraternity, but had also retained the cutting, uncultivated tone which many officers who had been in the war adopted towards civilians, all of whom they despised. The Puetters were, even then, such ardent Nazis that they refused to come to the wedding of a Jew. Ruth Puetter, however, a practical-minded woman, grasped very quickly that it was quite pleasant to visit her sister Edith and to let herself be pampered by her and to exploit the hospitality of her Jewish brother-in-law. After all he had been a major in the Medical Corps and had all the medals and decorations. One did not absolutely have to show him off to the Puetter family. She also seemed to be concerned that a boycott would cause my father to stop supporting her brother Jens as generously as he did.

With the Puetters and the other friends of my stepmother, the spirit of Prussia came to dwell among us and my father, who until then had defended himself gently against it, now yielded, step by step. He did nothing to defend me against his wife, not even when she tormented me.

I had always been chubby, with a pretty, lively face, but with short legs and arms. The fashion of the time favored slender, boyish figures: that was fine for my stepmother, but catastrophic for me. And I was only allowed to buy the cheapest clothes. Although I hated sewing, I still made a dress for myself, under the guidance of my girlfriend's mother, that looked fairly good on me and was in the sporting style that suited me best. A couple of times I got an evening gown, so that Mrs. Edith could show people how well she treated me. Naturally, I didn't want to wear those dresses out of spite and I deliberately ran around in sandals and hatless. My father supported his wife and shared her opinion that I was unattractively fat, to which I responded, "Better fat than elegant and ignorant, like your wife." Although, unlike my brother, I was visibly lacking in sex appeal, I suffered from no inferiority complexes whatsoever. Two friends of my brother, the law students Alfred Hoengen from a Catholic family in Aachen and Karl Fulda, son of the author Fulda and the son of the artist Kainer, visited us often. We went out together, admired Richard Strauss and Erwin Piscator, Hermann Hesse and Franz Werfel and went bicycling and swimming together. None of them ever so much as tried to kiss me.

Alfred and Karl made no effort to ingratiate themselves with my stepmother Edith. They made it clear that they preferred my company. During one of our many rows, Edith let herself go, saying, "You and your intellectual Jew boys!" I went to my father and told him, very coolly and deliberately this time: "If your wife doesn't like my friends, because they're intellectual and one of them is half Jewish, then from now on I won't bring them home; I'll meet them outside the house." This cool threat led to the only victory I ever won over my stepmother. My father not only apologized for his wife, but forced Edith to beg my pardon as well. But there was almost daily friction over the most ridiculous things: for example when I was expected to call Edith "Mama" or to kiss the hands of old ladies according to the custom in Prussian good society. My father did not dare to contradict his wife; neither did he have any arguments to contradict me, when I threw one of my temper tantrums. A few times he got palpitations; my stepmother would overdramatize these incidents and I would beg my father's pardon to calm him down.

Our discussions often took on a political character. Edith's remarks about my Catholic friends: "Catholics are treacherous. Only ignorant people are Catholic" unleashed a storm of opposition from me, not to mention her racist opinions: "It hasn't been proven that Christ was a Jew. There is evidence that he was the illegitimate son of a Germanic warrior", got me so worked up that I told the lady right to her face how stupid, ignorant and malicious she was.

At fifteen, I refused to continue attending the Lutheran religion class. Together with my Lutheran girlfriend, I visited a synagogue for the first time, simply to irritate my father and his wife. I am indebted to Max Seydewitz for my first real political quarrel with my father. Max was a Social Democratic deputy in the Reichstag and editor of an important party newspaper. He belonged to the left wing of the Social Democratic Party of Germany (SPD). Later his opposition to the reformist course of the SPD became so fundamental that together with Kurt Rosenfeld and Heinrich Stroebel he founded a new party, the Socialist Workers Party, which gained membership especially among the workers in red Saxony.

My parents took me to Seefeld in the Tyrol, for the Christmas holidays. They didn't ski themselves, but they didn't mind if I went skiing with some of the young people. On the very first evening, the son of Kurt Rosenfeld, who belonged to a leftwing student group, introduced me to the married couple Ruth and Max Seydewitz. I felt as if I had just come out of a stuffy parlor with plush furniture and pious proverbs on the wall and stepped into a huge, open, lively public square. Just in terms of external experience Seydewitz stood out among the solid middle class guests at the hotel. Tall, broad-shouldered, with a full head of disheveled black hair, prominent cheekbones and highly expressive facial features, he seemed, among the stiff, colorless citizens with their potbellies and bald heads, like a real man.

Despite numerous baleful stares by the other hotel guests Max came to dinner with his delicate, gentle looking wife, wearing a ski sweater or a sport shirt. As soon as the evening meal was done, I would move over to their table, where young Rosenfeld and other young people were already sitting. World affairs were loudly discussed, but there was a lot of laughter as well. My own democratic attitudes, which were hardly grounded in political knowledge, were a source of amusement for Seydewitz and he tried to teach me a few basic facts. His manner was to be sure somewhat condescending, but not pedantically didactic. I was so inspired by his wife that I would have been ready to do anything they might have asked of me.

The intellectually liberating atmosphere of the group surrounding Seydewitz was especially attractive to me because its exact opposite had developed at my father's table. Mrs. Edith had attached herself to a couple of overdressed Philistines in a standup collar and a chignon. Every evening we went through the same discussion because I refused to put on my evening gown to have dinner with the Captain Ret. and "Mrs. Captain". My father, to be sure, felt embarrassed when the Captain went on and on about his war experiences and toasted the Fatherland and its reawakening; but he also defended his wife when she became upset at my alleged intellectual arrogance.

Finally, on New Year's Eve, I refused to sit at the same table with my parents and their German Nationalist "idiots", as I called them and celebrated the New Year ostentatiously with toasts at Max Seydewitz' table.

CHAPTER III

1928 – 1933

Education – Secondary school in Berlin

"The Nazis had thrown a Jewish woman student out of the window of a lecture hall."

Lilli in her student days.

The next morning, during the ensuing confrontation, Mrs. Edith and my father upbraided me for supporting "the Reds" and I declared emphatically that it would be better for all concerned if I left home and went to a boarding school. My father agreed.

When we returned to Berlin, an acquaintance of my father's recommended a school on Lake Constance.

Gaienhofen, a country boarding school, is situated in a former castle on the German bank of the Untersee. This is the westernmost arm of Lake Constance, about a kilometer wide and the Rhine flows out through it. The opposite bank, with the little town of Steckborn, is in Swiss territory.

Gaienhofen was modeled on the ideas of the pedagogue Hermann Lietz and was progressive in the good sense, unencumbered by the rules of bourgeois etiquette and the Prussian spirit. The faculty tried to train us to be practical, civilized human beings. Of course, only well to do parents could afford a private school. They were people who had no time to take care of their children: artists or Germans living abroad, but also widows or divorced people. There were neither religious nor political conflicts: we grew up as if we were living on an island, far from the events of the world. Former Gaienhof students were rather unworldly. Some resisted National Socialism, but many others, once they had left the school, were so influenced by Nazi relatives and friends that they threw themselves quite uncritically into Politics and became active Nazi supporters.

The headmistress, Dr. Mueller, was in her fifties and in the time of the Kaiser had been the only woman to study mathematics at a German university. She was honest, upright, intelligent, free-thinking, but not an especially good mathematics teacher. The assistant headmistress, Dr. Haldimann, came from the Bern highlands in Switzerland. She was ardently democratic in her views and an excellent teacher: her history lectures were almost dialectical-materialist in method. She also understood how to teach literature in a new and exciting way. I recalled with horror the German classes of my last years in Berlin, conducted by a hardcore Nazi. In literature, we never got past Hebbel and Grillparzer. Instead we had to read the texts of entire Wagnerian operas and even learned selections from them by heart. These texts remained in my nightmares and today I still prefer to keep my distance from the operas of Richard Wagner.

HH, as we called Dr. Haldimann, not only made Goethe's Werther interesting, above all we read the most modern writers: Thomas Mann, Franz Werfel, Jakob Wassermann, Stefan Zweig. All six students in that class were stimulated in this way to read more books by good authors on their own initiative. At my request HH also recommended to me books by August Bebel and Maxim Gorky, which were in the library.

I didn't have close contact with my fellow students. They were older and more mature than I was and were not much interested in my political problems. My only closer tie to them was my passion for literature and theater.

On the other hand I felt very strongly drawn to my French instructor. The anti-French mood was especially pronounced in Prussia at the beginning of the 1920s and my girls secondary school in Berlin-Mariendorf was an experimental school, a so-called German High School, whose curriculum required the students to learn a Germanic language. In contrast to other schools, we had not started Latin and French in the fourth year, but had only taken English until our ninth year and then began Latin.

In order to qualify for my graduation certificate in Konstanz, the nearest city in the State of Baden, I had to make up eight years of French courses, within the next year and a half.

For that purpose I crossed over to Steckborn three times a week on the steamer to take private lessons in French. My teacher, Miss Rita Banderet, came from a Swiss-French family of teachers. She, her father and her brothers were not only known and respected as teachers, they were also Swiss patriots actively committed to the independence of their country. As a child Rita Banderet had been disfigured in an accident. When she realized that she probably would not marry, she adopted a little girl from Germany. I believe that it was only because of her warm heart and her temperament that she raised herself far above the narrow, restricted milieu of a Swiss small town. The responsibility of taking care of her adopted daughter, and her participation in the cultural and political life of her country had kept her from becoming a stereotypical old maid. She was a militant democrat, which in her case could be translated as "combative". After my experiences at home, discussions with Rita Banderet were a breath of fresh air. Although she certainly didn't intend it that way, my discussions with her were like signposts pointing the way to socialism. I learned from her that one must take the side of the people in the defense of democracy and not hide from the forces of reaction and fascism.

In order to improve my French, I spent the last two long vacations with a family in France. During this time I met my parents for a couple of days in Paris. They were en route to Biarritz, at that time one of the most elegant seaside resorts in Europe where, as my father told me with a muffled growl, they had taken a suite in one of the most elegant hotels. With two enormous trunks, Edith was well prepared for Paris and Biarritz.

On the second day of their stay they decided to dine at Prunier, an elegant restaurant especially beloved of German tourists. My father was wearing an inconspicuous dark suit. Edith wore an extremely smart tailored suit with an especially beautiful fox fur piece which she had just gotten as a birthday gift. My parents entered ahead of me; I stayed a few steps behind, in my cheap, out of fashion dress, sandals and without a hat. Frenchmen sitting at a table looked at my mother admiringly. One of them asked the other: "What nationality?"

His opposite number perked up his ears and answered "Germans".

"Oh la la," said the first one, "Germans and so elegant." At that moment I came into view and he added: "Ah, but the daughter, you can tell she's German ten miles away."

My father, who understood the exchange, turned red as a lobster and didn't dare to look at me. The next day, however, he commanded his wife to take me to a big department store and buy me a dress in which I could show myself in public.

During the meal at Prunier we talked about the situation in Germany, about the crisis, taxes and the general rise in prices. My parents declared that government policy was completely wrong and that the intolerable tax burden made it impossible to run a business. People in Germany couldn't lead normal lives anymore: no wonder they were moving their assets out of the country. I understood nothing about taxes or the flight of capital, but my sense of justice guided me. I told my father: "As long as you can buy your wife a fox collar for her birthday and can stay with her in the most expensive hotel in Biarritz and your twenty-one year old son can drive his own car, the taxes can't be all that terribly high. The money for unemployment compensation has to come from somewhere."

My father was speechless. Perhaps he agreed with me in his heart, but didn't dare admit it in front of his wife. He changed the subject and from then on he avoided all references to political and social matters. Later, in Berlin, he told my brother and sister, "It looks as if Lilli has fallen completely under communist influence at this boarding school." If the liberal Dr. Haldimann and Miss Banderet, the democratic Swiss woman, could have imagined that!

At Easter, 1931, I took my graduation examination before a State Board of Examiners. It was a so-called "wild" examination and was considered to be especially difficult because the teachers did not know the examinees and were unable to consider their normal accomplishments during the school year. In fact, two of our group of six students failed. I was more lucky than smart and my examination results were better than my schoolwork would suggest. In history, my favorite subject, my essay had caught the attention of the examiner and he informed me in solemn tones that he was going to test me for the highest marks. It sounded as if he were putting me on trial for my sins. The subject was "Social conflicts in the age of Bismarck and social achievements before and after the First World War." I couldn't have made a better choice myself. I poured out upon the examiners my entire knowledge of the German Social Democratic movement. Then came the question: what was I able to say about ecclesiastical efforts to achieve social betterment? My dismay must have been written on my face, because the examiners started laughing – although not at all in a mocking way. In fact, my Protestant upbringing and family connections helped me. I was able to say something about Protestant efforts, the Lutheran nursing orders and the Salvation Army.

"And what do you know about social currents inside the Catholic Church, about the papal encyclicals that concern themselves with social questions?"

"Nothing at all," was my prompt response. "I went to school in Berlin, in Prussia and, at best Catholics are looked down on there, but nobody takes them seriously," I answered rather rudely. A top grade now seemed out of the question.

Again, the examiners laughed. On my certificate, in history, I got a succinct "Very good": the highest grade possible.

We all agreed later with HH, that this was a proof of the democratic attitude of Catholic teachers. If the situation had been reversed and I had talked to a board of Prussian examiners about Catholic efforts at social reform and told them that I knew nothing about Protestant activities, I would barely have gotten a passing grade.

When I returned to Berlin, the debate recommenced about what course of study I should pursue. My first wish had been to become an actress, but my father had long since talked me out of it. I had to agree with his arguments, that it was a miserable life, unless I had a spectacular success; and besides I didn't have the right sort of figure. My acting talent was suited to tragicomic roles and I knew there weren't many of those. My father also energetically opposed my second wish, to study history or geography. "What can you do with that? Become a teacher? That's the only thing open to you and you're certainly not cut out to end up as a dried-out old maid."

And I too could envision myself turning into a conservative, nationalistic lady in a girls' high school, looking as if someone had taken her down from a shelf and forgotten to dust her off.

My father himself, although increasingly under the influence of his wife and constantly criticizing me, was fixated on the notion that I had the talent, the strength of character and the determination to become an outstanding travel writer. He suggested that I study journalism, after which he would finance my initial travels, until I had made a name for myself and would be able to work independently. Although my life at Gaienhof had been pretty remote from social reality, I was still able to see that this was no career for a single young woman.

After long discussions we decided that I would choose a course of study combining political economy with journalism. I also attended two courses of history lectures. Arthur Rosenberg was lecturing on materialist philosophy in the ancient world. I still remember these lectures as a brilliant introduction to dialectical materialism. Rosenberg, already a well-known historian, was only an unsalaried lecturer, a "Privatdozent". About a dozen students attended his lectures, who couldn't afford to pay the registration fee to attend lectures by the regular faculty. Since I was paying lecture fees, I got a voucher from Rosenberg stating that I had both enrolled in the course and paid for it.

"My God," he said, "a student who actually pays to hear me lecture. I haven't seen that in a long time." He smiled sadly. Since a Privatdozent did not receive a salary, but only lecture fees of two marks and fifty pfennigs per student per semester, it's easy to understand why, in Berlin at that time, his lectures were the only Marxist ones.

I don't know whether Arthur Rosenberg was able to live on his earnings as an author and journalist or whether he had private means sufficient for him to allow himself the luxury of being a Privatdozent.

The so-called required courses were given by professors who, when things went well, were not hostile to the Republic. Most of the students demonstrated their National Socialist or German

Nationalist opinions at every opportunity. One might say that the students worked more with their feet than with their heads. They stamped their feet to show agreement and shuffled them to show disapproval. If the professor said something politically or morally inflammatory, for example, "The English understood how to seize control of everything the Germans had built up in their colonies through hard and laborious effort," then there would be such a trampling, that the lecturer couldn't be heard. Or when he declared, that all civilized people kept their women out of politics and banished them to their place in the home, then the majority would stamp their feet, while there would vigorous shuffling at some of the benches. The right-wingers lumped the Socialist student group, the Pacifist Student League, the Centrist Catholic students and the Jewish students all together with the Communist students, under the collective name "the Commune" – which was meant as a term of abuse. The "Commune" only amounted to a fraction of the whole student body. In the student council, the Communist students had only four seats out of one hundred, while the reactionary students of the dueling fraternities had fifty-six seats. Nevertheless the little group was seen and heard everywhere: their leaflets were constantly being defaced on the bulletin boards, or torn down. During certain lectures they made their presence known by blowing trumpets, or loudly scraping their feet. Another reason that they were always so visible in the lecture halls was that their real opponents, the students of the dueling fraternities, didn't take their studies so seriously and only attended lectures sporadically. These sons of affluent families wasted their first semesters in the fencing room or in drunken parties and if they did finish their studies with poor grades, it was no big problem: the old boys' networks of their fraternities would make sure that they got good jobs.

I found my way to the leftist students soon after I started my first semester in Berlin. Early in May I experienced a major battle at the entrance to the University. On the afternoon of the previous day, the Nazis had thrown a Jewish woman student out of an upper story window of a lecture hall. She was taken to the hospital with serious injuries. A call to action immediately appeared on the bulletin board and the leftist students negotiated with a Jewish student organization, which declared itself prepared to fight alongside us in this case. Otto Hartwig, a member of the SPD, a nice boy from the Rhineland, alert and smart and Kassi Tennenbaum, whose mother was a Russian revolutionary and who looked as if he had just come from a leadership meeting of the Komsomol, both recruited me. We were about fifty students altogether, fewer than ten of us were girls. We assembled in front of the bulletin board of the Socialist and Communist students. Several were wearing insignia that indicated their Communist persuasion; others showed the three arrows, the symbol of the Reichsbanner, the Social Democratic fighting organization. The word was passed: absolutely no knives, just briefcases with heavy books; for the girls, pencils with sharpened points. A sharpened pencil, stuck into the arm of an opponent and broken off could, under the right circumstances, render a strong man "hors de combat."

Today I can still see the dark-haired Kurt Stern, with his prominent nose, in my mind's eye. Gaunt and upright, he always stood in the first row. The Nazis particularly had it in for him and on many occasions he served as a target. But he stood unshakable when the blows were raining down upon him. I remembered him as a bold, rough fighter – and thus I was all the more astonished when I saw him again in 1957 at a reunion of former Buchenwald prisoners: a spiritualized intellectual, not very robust; one couldn't imagine that he had ever taken part in a brawl.

Another tireless fighter who lives on in memory is Guenther Kiefert, a blonde athlete with an open, honest face. He assigned me to the left wing without asking many questions.

This time, because of our quick reaction and because we had succeeded in mobilizing a lot of people who were against the Nazis, we had the upper hand. We quickly succeeded in forcing the hostile groupings, among which a cluster of colored fraternity caps kept bobbing up, into the outer courtyard of the University. A group of young workers was standing on "Unter den Linden", unable to get through the closed gate and onto the campus. Somebody must have called the police, because they were standing in front of the gate with their rubber clubs, waiting for the combatants to be pushed out onto the street. At that time, police and other nonstudents could only enter the campus with special permission from the Rector. He held strictly to his academic independence and to the extra-territoriality of his institution. That was why the police stood by and watched the worst kind of fighting and did nothing. They were locked out. In especially serious cases an academic security service was organized, but it was completely dominated by German Nationalists and students from the dueling fraternities. That was how the University defended itself against the Republic.

After we had driven the enemy out onto "Unter den Linden", we wanted, together with the Young Socialists and the Rechsbanner students, to keep on chasing the Nazis. But we hadn't reckoned with Mr. Zoertgiebel's police. Within seconds they had formed a protective screen around the Nazis and any of us who tried to get closer got a taste of the rubber clubs. The Nazis marched off in formation, singing Fascist songs.

In the days that followed, the security service was increased and student identity cards were checked more carefully. Nevertheless new faces kept showing up in the corridors and in the lecture halls. We could see and hear that these were not really new students. However, because they had paid registration and lecture fees, they had valid identity cards. The fraternities had recruited a gang of hired thugs from among the unemployed.

We didn't of course, have the funds to buy that kind of protection. Our allies were locked out of the University. The most they could do was to cover our retreat, when we were driven off the campus and onto the street.

The financial situation of the leftist students was generally so catastrophic that at the end of the month they had to live on bread and tea. As bad as the food in the University cafeteria was, it still wasn't free, not even for scholarship students. Many students appeased their hunger at one of the Aschinger chain of cafeterias where, if you paid fifty pfennigs for a bowl of bean soup with fatty bacon in it, you could eat all the little rolls you wanted. Many a starving student stuffed himself at Aschinger's. And some days they had a special: bratwurst with cabbage and potatoes for seventy-five pfennigs.

Despite all political differences, my father found it quite natural for me to help fellow students who were in financial difficulties and to invite them home. At about one-thirty in the afternoon he would drive home from his clinic on Friedrich Strasse and stop on "Unter den Linden" to pick me up. Then I only had to say, "Papa, may I introduce Mr. Hartwig or Mr. Bergmann and Miss Holz?"

"Would you like to come to lunch? I'm driving back to town at 3:45 and I can bring you back," was my father's prompt reaction. The chauffeur would laugh sarcastically, especially when a poorly dressed young lady was involved. Ali Bergmann, who was a joker, would lay bets on whether this method of getting a free lunch would work and of course he always won. Many leftist students enjoyed my father's hospitality on a regular basis. My stepmother got used to this open house and in fact she preferred my friends, who were in their twenties, to the friends and relatives of my father, who were so much older. Of course we talked about politics and everyone was in agreement about the

Dr. Schlesinger's chauffeur driven car

threat of Nazism and that something effective had to be done about the steady growth of unemployment.

Opinions clashed only once during this time. I often ran into Lilli Fuchs, a fellow Gaienhof student, who was significantly older than I. She worked for the leftist press and moved in politically active circles opposed to the official leadership of the Social Democratic Party. Through her I first became acquainted with a leftist trade union official, a former metal worker who was solidly grounded in Marxism. Paul Krauter was about forty years old, a strong husky man with a lively, expressive face, merry light-colored eyes and short-cropped, slightly graying hair which gave his head a round look. I felt a lot of respect for him, because I quickly saw that he was well informed and his views were logical. He spoke to me in the familiar form, calling me "du", from the very first and treated me like a little comrade. When I was with him I controlled my smart Berlin mouth.

Because Lilli Fuchs and her betrothed had no money, my father offered to hold their wedding in our home. My stepmother got along well with Lilli, who was about the same age as she and organized a nice garden party to which about thirty guests, mostly young people, were invited. After dinner, my father's reliable instincts led him to Paul Krauter and the two of them sat together in a corner until two in the morning and talked. My attempts to tempt one or the other to leave their corner failed. Nor was the bride able to separate Paul Krauter and my father. As I was going to the train station with the bridal pair and Paul Krauter, Paul suddenly stopped. "I never would have thought that your old man was so reactionary – and he's really nice!"

On the other hand my father asked me, the next morning: "Who was that older man I was talking with?"

"Paul Krauter; he's a trade union officer," I answered.

"Well," he continued thoughtfully, "a lot of what he says makes sense and a lot of what he's asking for is justified. If people would just not always be so radical and not always want to change everything by force."

"Do you believe that the Fascists and reactionaries can be dealt with without force?" My father had no answer to that question.

In the summer of 1931 Lilli Fuchs introduced me to Professor Gumbel who taught economics and statistics at the University of Heidelberg and who in recent years had figured in more than one scandal. As early as 1925 the Minister of Education and Culture of the State of Baden had declared that Gumbel was "a marked man" whose right to speak before an academic organization had rightfully been denied.

Nationalist students armed with clubs had forced their way into a trade union meeting at which Gumbel intended to speak about the secret and illegal rearming and expansion of the German Army. Undaunted, he denounced the increasing political murders, the exoneration of political murderers by the justice system and the connivance of the political apparatus of the Republic in legalizing the Nazis. In 1931, Gumbel published a brochure commissioned by the League For Human Rights: "Let Heads Roll. Fascist Murders, 1924-1931." in which he set out irrefutable facts about political murder trials. This provoked demonstrations at the University. Everyone who tried to attend Gumbel's lectures was stopped by gangs of thugs and Gumbel himself was so badly beaten that in the summer of 1931 he could only walk with effort and with the aid of a cane. Gumbel was a brilliant, good-looking man of about forty, who regarded his situation with humor, but with no illusions. Those who were most responsible for the beatings at the University were not expelled, but Gumbel, at the beginning of 1932, under a Social Democratic Minister of Education, lost his professorship at the University of Heidelberg.

The National Socialist Students' League had conquered the "right" to fire professors. Gumbel went to France, where he was active in the anti-Fascist movement.

I had good friends among the leftist students and we took summer vacations together. My best friend, though, was Otto Hartwig, the only working class student in our circle. We frequently got together over tea, beer or lemonade at the digs of one of our fellow students, whose parents put a big room at our disposal. Until the wee hours we sang progressive songs or the chansons from the "Threepenny Opera" and recited poems by Weinert and Tucholsky. There was also a couple, who were necking in a corner, but that didn't bother me. The criticisms that I heard at home, about young girls indulging in such "dangerous" pleasures, left me cold.

Because I was sick and tired of the petty infighting with my stepmother, I went to Geneva for the next semester, to improve my French. There I fell seriously in love for the first time, with a Communist, of course. Louis Brecher was a Romanian Jew from Bukovina who had graduated from the Institute for International Law with full honors. He was not at all handsome: very tall, dark-haired with dangling locks, broad cheekbones and a high, arched forehead - a strongly chiseled, rather brooding face. But, as a brilliant speaker, he made a great impression on the workers and above all on the intellectuals of Geneva, in spite of, or perhaps because of, his accent.

During the winter Brecher directed, at the Workers' Theater of Geneva, Friedrich Wolf's "Potassium Cyanide", which was well received and not only by the workers.

With the help of my stepmother's connections, an apprenticeship was quickly found for me, for which, however, my parents had to pay the sum of one hundred fifty marks per month. That corresponded to the monthly wages of three female farm workers. My workday started at 5AM: stall inspection or preparing the payroll.

It ended at six in the evening when I came in from the field with the workers. My direct boss was Chief Inspector Huelsmann, a shrewd businessman and a trained agronomist with a lot of practical experience. The four thousand acre estate of Buselwitz in the district of Oppeln belonged to Mr. Peter von Wichelhausen, scion of an old aristocratic family which possessed still other estates in the area. The Weimar Republic had appropriated eight hundred million marks annually for the distressed areas in the eastern part of the country. This was the so-called "Eastern Aid" and most of it had been distributed among landowners with holdings of more than eight hundred acres. Despite this assistance, in 1930 Mr. von Wichelhausen was once again facing bankruptcy. The Agricultural and Industrial Bank in Oppeln, which had been established expressly for such cases, promised to save the estate by taking over the mortgages and paying out cash subsidies. The estate was known for its poor management and the bank required, as a condition of receiving Eastern Aid payments, that it employ a competent administrator. This administrator was Mr. Huelsmann. Two years after he took over the management, the estate was a viable operation and Mr. Huelsmann had purchased for himself, from his own earnings, a little farm in the most fertile part of Lower Silesia.

Huelsmann came from a middle class family in Westphalia. A tall, slender, good-looking man whose hair, at thirty-five, was already white. Elegance of attire was important to him and if I had met him in a restaurant I would certainly have thought he was a wealthy Rhineland industrialist.

Mr. Von Wichelhausen himself, after his marriage to a young noblewoman, had used the rehabilitation of his estate mainly to bring his own private finances and his castle up to the level which he found to be appropriate for a member of the Prussian Junker land owning class. He passed most of the year at the Hotel Adlon, near the Brandenburg Gate, at that time the most elegant hotel in Berlin. He also spent one or two months a year in Monte Carlo. He also spent a few weeks at his castle in Upper Silesia, during which time his main occupation was hunting. When Huelsmann tried to explain to him that game drives were especially damaging to the crops, the high and noble lord would become sulky with his steward and trustee. The Von Wichelhausens drove to Oppeln or Breslau in a chauffeured limousine. On the estate, Von Wichelhausen used a light hunting carriage, to which he hitched a pretty black horse. The young landowner did not, of course, find it necessary to climb down from the carriage when he had some small matter to discuss with Mr. Huelsmann. He didn't even climb down when Mrs. Huelsmann was present. He greeted me with a haughty nod of the head. He also nodded to Huelsmann's deputy and that was all. I believe the Wichelhausens would have taken it as an intolerable affront if they had to discuss some problem with one of the overseers, let alone actually see one of the field hands at the castle.

Mrs. Von Wichelhausen also played the grande dame on occasion. One fine summer's day she appeared in all her splendor at the Huelsmann home. Mrs. Huelsmann was wearing a pretty linen dress, whose belt had a big key ring hanging on it. "Oh," cried the grand lady, "how funny you look with your key ring, just like Grandmother's day!"

"I may look old fashioned, but when our grandmothers still carried their key rings on their belts, there weren't so many estates going bankrupt!" was the response of the smart and self-confident Mrs. Huelsmann.

Mrs. Von Wichelhausen left the house without saying a word and for some time relations were strained between the castle and the Inspector's house.

Huelsmann was frequently consulted as an expert in other Eastern Aid matters. From time to time he vented his anger and cursed the Junkers and their helpers among the nobility and the military. He complained about the misuse of Eastern Aid funds, which were used almost exclusively for the benefit of the big landowners. Although there were seven million unemployed workers in Germany, the estates continued to hire Polish farm hands to bring in the harvest. Huelsmann placed his hopes on a future National Socialist government that would put a stop to the practice, bring in Germans and push back the Poles.

I clearly recall his anger, when he returned one day from inspecting a nearby estate. The estate belonged to a retired general whose holdings were going to be put up for auction, unless the Industrial Bank took over his debts.

"I much prefer Peter von Wichelhausen," he said. "he stays in Monte Carlo and Berlin and at least he doesn't do any damage."

"But this general won't plant crops that have a good yield; he wants something that grows in orderly rows in the fields. He's got about a hundred pigs in his stalls and he's taught them to do military drill. He directs them with his walking stick and has them standing at attention and doing "eyes right" and "at ease" all day long. They don't put on any weight, of course and he wants his pig farming to be subsidized because it loses money."

Huelsmann really had made the Wickelhausen operation profitable. The estate workers, who took most of their wages in kind and who lived in estate housing, did not seem discontented. The living quarters of the estate workers in the eastern areas were indescribably primitive. I don't believe that one could have offered such cramped, dark, moldy cubbyholes to workers in Saxony or southern Germany.

I remember a foreman, a small man, bald, always unshaven, in ragged clothing who spoke german with such a thick Polish accent that I could barely understand him. He was an expert at his job and often explained to me what had to be done. One day I was supposed to take a message to him. I came into the kitchen, where three children were playing and a fourth lay in bed. A table, two benches, an un-shaded light bulb and a lot of bowls and pots on a shelf were the only furnishings. Although the wife was still under forty, she looked as if she were sixty.

She immediately shoved the pots in which she was cooking to one side and placed another pot on the shelf so that I couldn't see what she was fixing. The door to a second room stood open. Except for a stove, the only things there were beds and shelves. When I spoke to Mr. Huelsmann about my dismay at these living conditions, he said, "When we came here, this family was living with seven children in one unheated room and a kitchen. Now they've got two heated rooms and a closet and the biggest kitchen in the house. Since then this foreman isn't active in the local Communist group any more. And, I tamed the second Communist the same way: I sent the son to a milking course and now for the first time the family is earning enough that all of them, father, mother and children, have warm winter jackets and boots."

However, Huelsmann was not entirely convinced that he had really bought the foremen. And so, before the election in the autumn of 1932, he told the estate workers bluntly that he would turn off the electric power supply if anyone even thought about voting for the Communists.

Since the Catholic priest had preached against the godless Socialists during Sunday mass, quite a few votes were expected to go to the Catholic Centre Party. Huelsmann didn't like that either. On the Sunday before the election, he hitched up the wagon and invited his wife and Mrs. Von Wichelhausen to drive with him to the Lutheran church in order to show the estate workers the preferred religion.

The workers naturally tried to take home some grain or fodder from the field or the granary. Their official portion wasn't enough to feed their chickens and pigs. I was supposed to watch out and make sure that nobody carried away anything in the pockets of their clothing, or in the sacks that held their mid-morning snacks. Although I never inspected them and always looked the other way, the workers did not trust me and treated me as one of the gentry.

In August the grain was threshed in a big threshing machine. For days I had been performing the dirtiest work at the straw-baler. Now I fed the sheaves to the threshing machine, which was not so dirty but not entirely without its danger. The girl standing next to me was in the final stage of pregnancy. I went to the foreman who was assigning the women to their jobs and asked if the girl couldn't come down from the machine.

"Now that's a really smart idea," he said, with a wicked grin. "We tried that already. But when one of them has a big belly like that and there's no father, then she'll stay on the machine because she hopes something will happen and the brat will be born dead."

And in fact the girl worked on the machine throughout the forenoon; at noon she climbed down bathed in sweat and pale and went home alone. Next morning the newborn was a topic of conversation among the women. They were pitiless in their criticism of the young mother. "No diapers, no blankets. Her mother gave her a couple of old rags and her father said if she isn't back to work in a week, he'll kick her out."

Up until then I had only seen one baby, my niece, a well cared for child in a white nursery. Still, I did know that a child absolutely had to have something to wear. At the noon break I went to my room and got some things together that seemed useful: a couple of handkerchiefs, a package of cotton blankets, two linen shirts, a jar of cold cream, soap and a woolen shawl. While the others were already back at work, I brought the package over to the workers' quarters.

The girl, visibly younger than I was, was sitting at a table holding the tiny child to her breast. Red as a crab, it was wrapped in a flannel rag. Busy with the nursing child, the mother did not even look up when I entered. In the clean kitchen there were two stools and a sideboard and a couple of stoneware plates stood on the cupboard. A stand with wash pans and a blue jug was decorated with a knitted wash cloth. Two saints' pictures and a knitted flag were hanging on the wall. The child made a terribly wretched impression. I found it so ugly that I couldn't bring myself to say something good to the mother. Saying something like "I'm sure you can use this," and "I hope everything goes well," I handed her the package. She went into the next room, put the child on the bed, came back very slowly, opened the package, stared at it and began to cry. I took a hurried leave. The next day, during the breakfast pause, the women gave their reaction. "You made the girl happy, but she doesn't deserve it," said one of the older women. On the way to the threshing machine I overheard two other women talking. "That's city folks for you," said the first one. "No, that's rich folks, they get these crazy ideas," answered the second.

Hitler was named Chancellor of the Reich and the Reichstag burned down. On the estate, no one paid much attention. Another new government! The main thing was, people had work and could buy food and at least the most essential clothing. To be sure, one of the women expressed the hope that now someone would keep a closer eye on the "clothing Jews" and stop them from charging such high prices for their wares.

My father wrote me a long letter to say that I shouldn't worry, he had already been through a few changes of regime and the soup was always hotter when it was cooked than when it was served and things wouldn't turn out so bad! Besides, I was the daughter of a war veteran, who had won every possible sort of medal and volunteered a second time in 1916. I certainly had nothing to fear. In any case it was good that I had switched to agricultural science – there would certainly be no numerous problems there.

In March 1933 he wrote a codicil to his testament, in which he gave preferential rights to his thirty-three year old wife and which stated, "My wife must in any case be placed in a financial position which will enable her to live free of financial worry, while my children are able to support themselves." My brother, at that point in time, had still not passed his medical examinations.

Huelsmann was very pleased by the change of government. He believed that the Nazis would pursue the policies which they had campaigned on while they were in opposition. Until the end of January they repeatedly threatened to investigate the whereabouts of the Eastern Aid funds.

Huelsmann's wife knew, however, that certain big industrialists who were close to Goebbels had supported the Agricultural and Industrial Bank before the takeover of power. Goebbels' friends had made loans, although the most incompetent aristocrats were among the Bank's directors. It was well known that Hindenburg's son had embezzled funds, organized fraudulent auctions and cheated small artisans out of their just demands for payment. At the end of 1933 the Nazis had threatened to bring the embezzlement of the Eastern Aid funds and the machinations of Hindenburg's son before the Reichstag. Later it was revealed that Hindenburg had made a deal with the Nazis: he would agree to appoint Hitler as Chancellor and the Nazis would drop the proceedings against his son. After the new regime came to power, the words "Eastern Aid Scandal" disappeared from its vocabulary.

CHAPTER IV

1933

Death of Father – Life in Paris

*"In March the Nazis called for a boycott of Jewish
businesses and Jewish doctors and attorneys."*

I am only able to reconstruct events in my parents' home during this time on the basis of oral reports and letters. Strangely, I had bad forebodings and twice I telephoned Berlin and asked my father if I shouldn't come for a weekend. He refused categorically, telling me that I should think about nothing but my apprenticeship.

In February 1933 Edith's brother joined the Storm Troopers and did, in fact, get a job after five years of unemployment. Until then, he had been a guest at our home two or three times a week and came and went in my sister's home and had also been a frequent guest in her summer cottage; but now he broke off all relations with our family from one day to the next. My sister and brother-in-law were not unhappy about this, because after the Reichstag fire they had offered asylum to some left Social Democrats and to some friends who were politically compromised.

My father, however, appeared deeply hurt. The different codicils to his will, which he composed in the months of February and March, showed us later that he was thinking about suicide even then. A passage indicated that he believed his wife would join him.

In March the Nazis called for a boycott of Jewish businesses and Jewish doctors and attorneys, for the first of April. My father shared his private clinic with Dr. Bruno Wolff, an ardent German Nationalist, who belonged to a Jewish organization with Fascist tendencies. He welcomed the Nazi government as an authentic German government and assured my father, that the boycott would not apply to them. It would only apply to unscrupulous business people and Jews from the East. Deserving German Jewish officers would not have Storm Trooper guards posted in front of their clinic.

On March 24 my father wanted to use the telephone. All the telephones in the upper story of the clinic were in use, so he went downstairs to the kitchen area, where there was another telephone. On the stairs he heard a kitchen employee, who had worked in the clinic kitchen for more than fifteen years, talking on the telephone and saying, that she hoped a really tough guard would be posted in front of the clinic on April 1 and keep everybody away and they ought to post a sign, to warn the people. They had to show the Jew who was the boss and that they didn't have any rights. My father confronted her and she began sobbing and insisted that she wasn't talking about him, but just about Dr. Wolff, because he was so awful and treated the employees with such contempt. In any event, this scene made such an impression on my father, that on the same evening he added a further codicil to his will, to the effect that the kitchen staff of the clinic should not be present at his funeral.

On March 31 Dr. Wolff reassured my father once again, that veterans of the war would be exempted from the boycott against the Jews. Despite that, my father sent his chauffeur to the pharmacy with prescription for morphine. On the morning of April 1 he went to his room to work, as he always did. At about 7:30, the chauffeur brought him the morning paper. The headline read "Storm Troopers To Stand Guard In Front Of All Jewish Firms – No Exceptions".

It was never established just how he had injected the morphine. He was found in his room by Mrs. Edith, of all people, who normally never got up before breakfast. She called my brother-in-law and my sister, who almost knocked down the Storm Troopers in front of their home, who wanted to check their papers. My sister drove through all the traffic signs, but it was too late and my father died that night.

My brother and I reached Berlin 48 hours later. Edith, who in order to secure the release of the body had negotiated very self-assertively with the police and had already done everything else that was necessary, now sat bathed in tears. My sister and my brother-in-law had their own problems. Only my brother tried to console me a little. At that time he was working as an intern at a Catholic hospital in Cologne. He hadn't had any problems there as yet. However, several of his politically left friends had been in danger and he had used his car to bring two scientists who were being sought by the Gestapo over the border. He had a smart little sports car. With the prettiest and blondest of his girlfriends next to him and the two fugitives in the rumble seat, he drove completely unmolested over the Dutch border on a Sunday morning.

The ladies from the clinic kitchen came to the funeral in their mourning garments. The family council had decided that it would not be opportune to accede to my father's wish. I was the only one who refused, demonstratively, to shake hands with the two women, whereupon one of them broke into loud sobs and the other wiped her tears. I had the impression that my gesture found a positive reception among some of the clinic staff, as they shook my hand warmly and repeatedly.

Mr. Jens Albrecht didn't once express condolences to us, but the Puetters, Edith's sister and brother-in-law, did come to Berlin to support her. I am sure that they sincerely regretted my father's death; still, that did not stop them from remarking, in casual conversation, that there were superior and inferior races. Herbert's prompt response was, "If there are superior races, then the German race certainly isn't one of them: the Germans are the mongrel product of tribal migrations."

Dr. Puetter left the room seething with rage and I laughed so hard that they had to remind me that I was in a house of mourning.

In general, the behavior of our non-Jewish friends was touching, regardless whether they were embarrassed democrats or leftist sympathizers. The friends of my brother and many of his former girlfriends and also many of my former classmates visited us or wrote letters expressing their outrage at the events during the Jewish boycott. The superior court judge, Dr. Erich, father of my oldest girlfriend, was among these.

The family of my father, on the other hand, was filled with pity for poor pitiable Edith. They outdid one another in expressions of sympathy and forgot their own problems, which they may not have regarded as quite so tragic. I was politely eased out of the picture: my father and Edith in particular had complained to everyone about my leftist tendencies and my Communist friendships. It was also known, that in February my father had written a codicil to his will, stipulating that neither my brother nor I were to have control of our portions of the inheritance before reaching age 35. "That's so you don't give yours to the Communists and I don't spend mine on chocolate" my brother explained. He said aloud, what the others thought.

My brother-in-law Dr. Freudenthal was appointed my guardian, since I was not yet twenty-one and thus still a minor. He did not interfere with my freedom of decision and did not condemn my leftist ideas, on the contrary. There was no longer any chance of my being allowed to pursue my studies in Germany. I decided to go to France. Fritz Freudenthal helped me with references.

The family was glad to get rid of me. Especially Mrs. Edith, who in the meantime had entered into relations with a "friend of the family", an SS man. He found it desirable to restrict to a minimum her meetings with the uniformed guest, who clicked his heels with a hearty, "Heil Hitler!". She very kindly supported my departure.

I traveled to Paris with my sister in the autumn of 1933. For her, it was a vacation trip. Those who weren't being politically persecuted thought that the situation could still be normalized. My sister had a few acquaintances, artists, journalists and doctors and in Paris we met a friend of the family: court counselor Broh, who had defended Max Hoelz. He was already almost seventy and had been active for the Red Cross organization – an old gentleman who had been taken by the Storm Troopers and terribly abused. They had let him go mainly because his elegant, sixty - five year old wife had succeeded in making contact with people at the highest level in order to save her husband.

My brother-in-law's brother, Kurt Freudenthal, was very helpful. He had been a popular dentist in the Ruhr area, who had never made a secret of his sympathy for the workers and Communists. For that reason, his practice had already become a target for the Nazis in February 1933. The harassment to which he was subjected included house searches, confiscation of materials and verbal and physical attacks on his patients. At the beginning of March he fled to Paris with his technician, Leo Schubert, a young Communist and his partner, another politically committed dentist.

His patients and employees had helped him and Schubert to take most of their instruments and materials with them. Schubert had opened a dental laboratory semi-officially and under a French name and Freudenthal had an illegal practice.

Things were very hard for doctors and lawyers in the emigration because they were not officially allowed to practice. Thanks to various recommendations, especially from high-ranking police officers and parliamentarians whom he had treated for free, Kurt

Freudenthal's waiting room was always filled with patients. The more influential Frenchmen, whom one recognized by their dark, well-cut suits and the rosette of the Legion d'honneur in the button hole, received preferential treatment, of course. Freudenthal knew how to avoid all unnecessary pain, but he kept his patients coming back, especially when the work of his outstanding technician was called for. The German emigrants met in his waiting room and a friend used to say that a root canal with Kurt Freudenthal was a lifetime appointment. Kurt, shorter and less handsome than his brother Fritz, with short graying hair and thin lips, shared his brother's ability to inspire confidence in his patients. He had brought his receptionist along from Germany, a blonde young woman whose good looks were equaled by her intellectual limitations. She was visibly troubled by the "Jewish-Bolshevik atmosphere"; still, she had followed her boss to Paris. Later, during the war, when Kurt, as a German, had been interned by the French, there was an Englishwoman, a consular employee, who drove out to the internment camp once a week to bring him a package – a circumstance which we also made use of, to help our friends. Thanks to a young, pretty Australian woman who married him, he was evacuated from France with the English troops.

Kurt's patients advised me about my studies and I learned that, with my German diploma, I could be admitted to the agricultural college of the University of Toulouse.

CHAPTER V

1934 – 1937

University of Toulouse – Jascha

"There was no longer any chance of pursuing my studies in Germany. I decided to go to France."

A nd so I began to study there in November 1933. We had to follow a set curriculum during each year of study and at the end of that time we had to pass examinations in almost all subjects, which were graded on a scale of zero to twenty. At that time, there were a fairly large number of foreigners in the provincial universities. There were a number of students from the Balkan countries and Poland; they had received French diplomas in their own countries and came from well to do families. The Bulgarians and Yugoslavs were an exception. Many of them were Communists and were working their way through the University with a variety of outside jobs. A lot of Algerians were studying at Toulouse. At the college of agriculture they were mostly the sons of big landowners, who wanted to get acquainted with "the big world" in France. Their freedom consisted primarily in the fact that here they could keep a mistress, drink alcohol in cafes and nightclubs and look at the scantily clad girls. Of course they cut the morning lectures. During my final year at the University I was able to earn a bit of money by writing bachelor's theses for the laziest among my Egyptian fellow students. One of the Egyptians had, during his first semester, started a serious relationship with a Romanian student. The young lady, daughter of

a prominent government official in Bucharest, was not only intelligent and eager to learn, but also extremely energetic. She compelled her friend, the son of an effendi, to regularly attend all the
lectures and to work so hard for his exams, that he passed almost
all of them with a grade of "good".

We were four girls among twenty-five young men, the Romanian,
a very plain French girl, a Vietnamese princess and me. The Vietnamese princess looked like a porcelain doll, delicate, slender,
with big black eyes and always a friendly smile. In the practical
courses there was always an assistant or a mechanic, who would
carry heavy objects for her, or lift her up onto the antediluvian
tractor that we were supposed to drive and then run alongside
holding the steering wheel. She spoke no French whatever. But
when, in oral exams, she lisped out a few sentences and nodded
her head as if to confirm what she had just said, the examiner,
after a few admonitions, would let her through every time with
an eight or a nine. The only exam she failed was chemistry with
a blind examiner.

On my second day, a student spoke to me in German. A stocky,
healthy looking fellow with a round head. He introduced himself
as Sascha Bikowski, a Latvian brought up in Germany. He had
studied agriculture on a Jewish estate, where a group of young
Zionist Jews were preparing themselves for emigration to Pales-
tine within the setting of a so-called Hachschara. Bikowski, however, wanted to earn a degree in agricultural engineering. He
asked me at once if I was a Zionist. When I said I wasn't and confessed that I didn't even know what a Hachschara was, he shook
his head disapprovingly. But we continued to exchange friendly
greetings and to discuss student affairs.

Hardly a week had gone by when I found him waiting for me after
a lecture. Standing next to him was a blond young man with a narrow head, a long, sharply curved nose and rather high shoulders. In
his blue-grey knickerbockers and worn windbreaker you could spot
him as an intellectual from a long way off.

First impression: a Russian-Jewish student out of a film. Sascha introduced him as Jakob, nicknamed Jascha. He was studying the biology of industrial fishing. He had also grown up in Germany, but came from a Lithuanian family.

I really can't say that it was love at first sight. Jascha told me later that Sascha showed me to him on the street and said "Come on, we can catch up with her," to which he replied "I'm not running after that cow!".

We went to a cafe together. Ten minutes later we were so deep into conversation that we forgot Sascha was there. I invited them to eat supper the next evening in my room, where I had a spirit cooker and some dishes. The first time Sascha came along, but since the conversation turned into a dialogue between Jascha and me, he began meeting us for lunch in a small cheap restaurant.

During the first evenings we began sharing out family histories. Jascha came from a good Jewish family; his father was both a committed and a conservative Zionist. He had been a business-man in St. Petersburg and had settled with his family in Koenigs-berg in 1919, while his relatives and the business remained in Lithuania. The family had Lithuanian passports, but at home they only spoke Russian. At sixteen, Jascha had, to the conster-nation of his father, joined a radical left Zionist youth group, which he left after completing school to join the Red Student League and, soon after that, the Communist Party. In 1932 his parents wanted to be naturalized in Germany, but German citi-zenship was denied them on account of the "Communist subver-sion" of their son Jacob.

Great outrage in the family. "You're going to turn out like your cousin Red Michael in Moscow, who regards the whole family as dead," lamented his mother.

Jascha went for a semester to Berlin and in the winter of 1932 to Munich, where he was active in the Communist Party; this resulted in his being expelled from both universities. By the spring of 1933 he was in such danger that he was sent to Paris. He worked in the organizational bureau of the "World Congress of Youth Against War and Fascism". How enthusiastic he was, when he told me about working with Alfred Kurella! Kurella, a professional politician and author, knew how to inspire his youthful collaborators. Under his intelligent, non-bureaucratic management the young people accomplished nearly impossible things during the congress.

Jascha's parents, meanwhile, had left Germany and were safe in Lithuania. All the Communist activities were now forgiven and forgotten and Jascha's Papa was now ready to pay for his son to recommence his studies in France. Jascha got official permission from the Party to go to Toulouse with the mission of working at the University for the German anti-Fascists group, making contact with leftist French students, distributing materials and information to them and also to German émigrés and above all collecting signatures and money among progressive professors.

From the very first moment Jascha was my political mentor and I had unlimited confidence in his intellectual superiority. After only two weeks he started giving me practical work to do. We reached a sort of sponsorship agreement with a Communist youth group, which later helped political émigrés.

I also began to collect signatures for the anti-Fascists manifestocs among the professors and assistants. We had the most success among the medical faculty, due to Camille Soula, a Catalonian with connections to leftist circles in Barcelona who had a lot of political influence among his colleagues. Professor Ducuing also helped us. He held the chair for surgery and was considered the best surgeon in the whole of southern France. In contrast to his reactionary colleagues he was an ardent Socialist and an intimate friend of the Social Democrat and later of President Vincent Auriol.

Professor Ducuing had already, in the summer of 1933, hired a persecuted German physician to work in his laboratory. He also hired a German woman, a Communist, to look after his grandchildren. In contrast to most doctors Ducuing came from very modest circumstances. He had quite literally fought his way through his studies with stipends and part-time jobs.

In 1934 he also owned his own private clinic and could charge whatever fees he wanted. He did this deliberately. Thanks to the rich snobs who believed that they had to have their appendix removed by him and only by him, he was able to treat poor patients and destitute emigrants for free. His colleagues feared him, because he publicly censured every mistake and pilloried medical incompetence in all its forms. Until the beginning of the war he gave free treatment to all the comrades whom we sent to him. After the occupation of France, he not only treated the illegal comrades whom we sent him, without charge, but also organized places for them to hide. He had attended a congress in the Soviet Union in 1935 and on his return he gave a talk about his trip in the biggest auditorium of the University. He talked about the organization of medical care in the USSR and about the rights of the patients and the responsibilities of the doctors.

At the end of his talk he declared himself ready to join the Communist Party of France. He kept this promise. During the war he continued his fight against the Fascists and his aid to the Communists with real courage and during the last two years of the war he was forced to leave Toulouse and the clinic.

The agricultural faculty was generally reactionary, with the exception of the professor of forestry, Gaussin, and the professor of viticulture and deputy director of the institute, Louis Rives. Rives, the son of an estate inspector of modest means, had completed his studies by dint of ability and diligence. He did not forget his origins. He requested tuition waivers for the Bulgarian Communists and found good paying jobs for the leftist émigrés during vacation times.

Before long Jascha and I were spending our free time almost exclusively with each other. Common interests, aversions and sympathies and our enthusiasm for sports were a bond between us. We soon formed friendships with some of the other German émigrés who had ended up in Toulouse, but I felt unconditional trust and camaraderie only for him. He had already, back then, begun to call me affectionately "Teddybear", because, he said, I was cuddly and funny and friendly. I'm still called by this term of endearment today, after fifty years of marriage with him and many of our friends don't even know my real name.

Toulouse is in the South of France, in a region where oleanders and laurels and even palm trees grow in sheltered locations. Nonetheless, January 1934 brought an unprecedented cold spell to southern France, with temperatures of minus ten and minus fifteen degrees centigrade.

Entire vineyards and orchards did not survive that winter. We were living in furnished rooms, which were only heated by a fireplace. Double glazing was unknown in this region. Stone floors, canopies that provide shade and drafts are found in the best houses because they provide cooling during the long hot summers. Here, as in Italy, people seem to forget from one year to the next that there is such a thing as winter.

At the University, iron stoves were installed in the lecture rooms so that the professors could warm their hands. The students, shivering in their overcoats and gloves, endured heroically. Neither Jascha nor I had a warm room, so in the evenings we would meet with three or four other students in a café where we were warmed and cheered by hot grog and a fine gypsy band.

Contrary to conventional belief, morality in provincial France at that time was very strict. Almost all the female students who came from outside Toulouse lived in a dormitory. They had to be back in the dorm by eight o'clock at night. Once a week they went to the cinema as a group and the eldest and most Catholic of them was in charge of the key to the house and had to keep the flock together. Married couples went to the cafés, or ladies who were clearly sitting there for reasons of trade. The fact that I ran around without a hat was considered as almost exhibitionistic and the excitement resembled the moral indignation that a young girl in a miniskirt or trousers would have aroused twenty years ago in the Georgian capital of Tbilisi.

The professor of botany at the institute, an especially small-minded and limited pedant, told my fellow students, "Mlle. Schlesinger does not appear to be a serious young lady: I have seen her sitting in a café in the evening with a group of young people and she was not wearing a hat!"

When our protector Professor Rives heard about this, he asked my future husband not to make a scandal and to blame the stupidity of his colleague for this silly chatter.

In February 1934, on a bitterly cold evening, Jascha brought me home at midnight. At the door I found I'd forgotten my house key. I had no choice but to go to his room to sleep. After this night we were inseparable. At the beginning of the following month we rented a big room together. Of course that became known immediately and at the University we were regarded as officially engaged.

We were almost never invited to the homes of French people, not even in progressive circles. The middle classes in the South were very reserved. Even a Parisian would almost never enter the homes of his colleagues and friends in Toulouse. People would meet in a restaurant. During the four years that we spend in Toulouse, we were only invited to lunch one single time – at the residence of the director of the mental hospital, for whom Jascha had done some specialized photography.

Rives, the professor of viticulture, had no laboratory experience. Jascha had both knowledge and a technical flair and set up the laboratory for him; he also trained me as a laboratory assistant. In the spring, while the vines were in bloom, we undertook a series of experiments, in the course of which we had to take samples in the field every two hours, during two days and nights. We took a couple of blankets and camped out in a shed in a vineyard owned by the University and did the work in turns. The alarm went off! The conservative director of the institute, Professor Nicolas, known to the students as St. Nicholas because of his white beard, summoned his deputy Rives. "These two might be German spies! What are they doing at night outside of town? Mlle. Schlesinger is a German – you need to be more careful. Besides, these students associate with Socialists and Communists."

Rives did not let himself be intimidated and recounted the story with an appropriate commentary, so that the whole University laughed.

During the summer vacation Jascha and I went to Paris, where he introduced me to some comrades from the student committee. I was given some errands to carry out on my trip to Berlin. During my absence, Jascha worked on a fishing boat in the North Atlantic.

It was easier to make contacts in Berlin than I had thought. The comrades were able to lead their usual lives, even Peter Frank, the son of a well-known professor of chemistry. He had been imprisoned in a concentration camp in 1933, but released after his father intervened. It appeared that the Nazis were, at that point, persecuting workers and the trade unions. Apparently they were hoping to win over the middle-class youth and the intellectuals.

I was astonished to see how unafraid the comrades were of making contact with me, of giving me material and information and indeed of introducing me to other comrades. People told jokes about the Nazis and passed on reports from the factories, where the old trade union officials held the most important positions, although not the leading positions, in the newly established Labor Front. I was told that in the working class district of Wedding, on the first of May, most of the balconies had been decorated with red feather beds which had been hung out "to air". My women friends and even my stepmother, gave me hints of a certain amount of opposition in officers' circles. Until 1935 people had been hoping for a return of the German Nationalist old guard. But after 1936, they began to adapt themselves completely to Hitler.

At the end of summer vacation Jascha and I travelled to Strasbourg. There we met the publicist and literary critic Max Schroeder who, as a Communist, had collaborated on the "Brown Book", a documentary denunciation of the Reichstag arson trial and who occasionally wrote for a German-language magazine in Alsace. Max wanted to know everything about my stay in Nazi Germany. While we savored our spiced wine, we discussed the political situation until late into the night. Max understood how to analyze my very narrow-gauge observations and to explain the background of political events to us. In a few evenings with Max I learned more than from many longwinded directives of the student committee.

In the spring of 1935 we decided to marry; above all because it greatly simplified both our trips to Germany and the situation at the University. Through marriage I could become a Lithuanian, if I renounced my German passport. That was a significant gain in security, but it came with financial problems. My parents-in-law were not happy about our marriage: I was a girl from an assimilated family with no sense of tradition and a Communist as well and we were marrying before completing our studies. However, they resigned themselves to the fact, especially after we visited them in Lithuania and it turned out that I was actually quite presentable. My sister-in-law admitted that the family had been greatly concerned that Jascha's wife would show up in a dirndl dress with sandals and her hair in braids, a real Germanic type.

My sister and brother took the attitude: "What counts is that you're happy together." Only the pious Jewish executor of my father's will, a cousin of my mother, declared that he represented my parents and first had to be satisfied that this boy was not marrying me to get his hands on my money.

I drew his attention to the fact that the money transfers to me had stopped during the last few months and that we were living on Jascha's monthly remittances from home and on his earnings as a photographer.

Thanks to our Lithuanian passports we were able to travel with relative freedom in Germany and we made plentiful use of this circumstance to make contacts and transmit messages. Only once did the police summon us for serious questioning: in the Lithuanian language masculine names end in -is: a married woman's name ends in -iene. The name in my husband's passport was Jacob Segalis; the name in my passport was Lilli Segaliene. It took us an entire forenoon to make this clear to the police in Berlin. On our honeymoon in Switzerland we were hauled out of our hotel room at five in the morning for the same reason by the morals police, who demanded to see our marriage certificate.

In 1935 and 1936 our assignments took us to the Rhineland. There was a strong anti-Nazi mood there, even in middle class circles which had previously been neutral and a young doctor, who had belonged to the Socialist students, told us that for the first time his Catholic family supported his political work. Many parents were refusing to let their children join the Hitler Youth.

Although Dr. Erich, the father of my best friend, was still working as a high official in the Ministry of Justice, we were officially residing with his family. There, too, people criticized the government and condemned an uncle who had joined the National Socialists. My friend Ursula, a music student, had become engaged to a young Catholic and, to the distress of her parents, was about to convert to Catholicism herself. Ursula did not feel that her Protestant education had given her a sense of moral stability and that we, with our radical views, had driven the moderate people into the Nazi camp.

Catholicism was the only force that could stand up to Fascist barbarism. Ursula was of course ignoring the fact that the Vatican, the highest authority of the Church, had long since made its peace with the Nazis. Ursula's younger, eighteen year old sister Erika, on the other hand, openly expressed her hatred for the Nazis. She had already experienced a whole series of unpleasant incidents because of her friendship with a Jewish boy, with whom she was seen in public. In the spring of 1939 she wrote to me from England. She had followed her Peter into the emigration and had married him despite all the obstacles. Her father and sisters broke off all correspondence with her.

We found it easy to organize our work with the intellectuals, but making contact with workers was difficult. For example, my husband was given the assignment of seeking out a young Catholic worker in Guetersloh. With the best will in the world we couldn't come up with a reason for a Lithuanian student to go to Guetersloh. The police were bound to become suspicious as soon as he checked in at a hotel. Jascha's enthusiasm for bicycling gave us the solution. He rented a bicycle in Duesseldorf and began a tour through northern Germany. At a prearranged time he organized a "breakdown" near Guetersloh, so that he had to spend the night in the local youth hostel. It turned out that the hostel was a neutral location and made a good meeting place.

Before our trips I had practically never been in the northern or eastern parts of Berlin, where the workers lived. However, I got the assignment of giving the wife of a leading comrade, who was ready to emigrate, a large sum of money and information.

I sent a letter to a cover address and got a postcard in reply, telling me to wait outside a movie theater on Memhard Strasse just before seven in the evening. I was supposed to have a French newspaper in my hand. When I showed up, just before seven, in a simple summer dress, wearing sandals without stockings, I was very surprised to see several heavily made-up ladies in high heels in the vicinity of the movie house. Not being a very good observer, I couldn't understand what they were waiting for. I knew, though, that I had to wait for the end of the film, so that my contact and I could blend into the crowd coming out. So I started sauntering back and forth, quite inconspicuously as I thought. But the ladies thought differently. "What's the country girl doing here? Is that supposed to be the new look? She must be waiting for her man!"

Even then I didn't catch on; I got nervous and moved as far away from the movie as I could and stood in front of a store window. When the moviegoers began to pour out onto the street, I unfolded my French newspaper. Immediately I caught a final remark:" You got it wrong, Lisa, that's an intellectual!"

The comrade spotted me at once in the crowd and joined me and we walked off together in the direction of Friedrichsheim. I told her about my concerns. She laughed and said, "Oh, those are the hookers from Alexander Platz; they're not going to snitch to the cops."

As time passed, working with the intellectuals became harder. Diethelm Sheer, an assistant professor at the Institute of Fishery Biology at the University, had been arrested, along with two students. Instructions from Paris, to work inside the Labor Front and the Nazi organizations and to infiltrate our cadres there, were regarded by some of the comrades as a provocation.

My stepmother left on a trip at the beginning of summer 1936 and closed her house, so together with my brother we rented an apartment, where we felt very safe and where we could also meet with our comrade Peter Frank. My brother's current girlfriend Dorlies was living with us. She was an attractive but shy and inhibited young Swiss woman. She was the only one of my brother's girlfriends with whom I didn't get along and on top of everything else she was afraid of Socialists and Communists.

At the beginning of August we came back from a trip and found Dorlies quite upset and Peter, unusually for him, worried. What had happened? At the end of July Peter Frank had shown up at the apartment, saying: "I'm Professor Frank's son. You know me well. I got back from vacation earlier than my parents and I don't have a key for their apartment. Your sister told me once that I could stay here."

"No problem," my brother answered. Dorlies thought it odd, that Peter stayed indoors all day and only went out late at night. After about four days my brother met a friend who lived in the same building as the Franks. "Guess who's staying with us at the moment," said my brother. "Peter Frank."

"Oh, so you're hiding him." came the answer. "The Gestapo has been sitting in the Franks' apartment for a week, waiting for Peter. I'd like to know how his parents managed to warn him."

Dorlies threw quite a fit. Peter, she insisted, had to clear out. Two days later my brother drove him out of Berlin in his car. A week later, as a tourist, he crossed the Alps into Austria.

In middle-class circles a new threat had arisen, from children and young people who were being systematically incited at school and trained to be informers.

Real dramas were played out in families because a daughter betrayed her father, or a little brother turned in his older siblings. Just within my circle of acquaintances alone there were three cases in which the person who had been betrayed and arrested committed suicide. In 1937 we were invited to dinner by Peter Frank's parents. After the meal we wanted to listen to Radio London. Suddenly Peter's little brother appeared in his pajamas and announced resolutely: "You know we're not supposed to listen to foreign broadcasts when we have visitors!" and went over to the radio and turned it off. We were so stunned, that we didn't dare turn the radio back on.

My stepmother had her own problems with her Nazi relatives. The name Schlesinger sounded too Jewish. In 1937, probably through her brother-in-law's connections, she obtained a certificate from Hans Globke, a high-ranking official in the Reich Ministry of the Interior, to the effect that Mrs. Edith had declared, in lieu of oath, that the marriage with my father had never been consummated in the five years they were together. Therefore she had remained a purely Aryan woman, was permitted to renounce the name Schlesinger and resume her former name.

Hans Globke had been one of the jurists who composed the commentary to the so-called Nuremberg Laws, the notorious Nazi racial laws. Later, in the Federal Republic of Germany, under Konrad Adenauer, he was a Permanent Under-Secretary in the Office of the Federal Chancellor.

From that day on I broke off all relations with Edith. I saw her only when we met at the office of the executor of my father's estate and then I used the formal mode of address when speaking to her. My siblings didn't take the matter so tragically, because she behaved quite decently toward them and even helped my brother and sister to emigrate. I actually didn't resent this gesture of hers as much as I did a letter I got from her in 1946, in which she wrote, how often she had thought about me and how happy she was that I had survived. That letter really offended me. She signed the letter "Edith Schlesinger". She not only took back the name Schlesinger, in 1947 she began receiving a pension as the widow of a victim of Fascism.

At this time our most important liaison man in Paris was the chairman of the illegal Communist Youth Association of Germany, comrade Artur Becker, ""Atze" to us. We called him the Golden Boy, because we respected and loved him. We would have walked through fire for him. He was a typical Rhinelander, inspiring confidence, humorous in a gentle way, blonde, of medium height, with chiseled features and clear, wise, friendly eyes. His stories were hilarious, but often instructive as well. Unlike some others his assessment of the situation in Germany was realistic, without lapsing into pessimism. He listened with interest to our stories about the danger of Goebbel's propaganda, constantly hammering so many lies into peoples' minds that some of it was bound to stick and he was concerned about the dangerous indoctrination of the children. Even today I feel a stab of pain in my heart when I think of him. In Spain he was a commissar in the International Brigades. At the Ebro he was seriously wounded and fell into the hands of the Fascists and was murdered by them.

CHAPTER VI

1937 – 1939

Protest

*". . . children and young people . . . were being trained
to be informers. A daughter betrayed her father,
or a little brother turned in his older siblings."*

We really led a privileged life in France. In 1937, after completing his studies, Jascha got the opportunity to work for Professor Henry Pieron at the College de Paris, in a laboratory dedicated to the study of the physiology of sensory perception.

Henry Pieron and his wife were democrats, who worked closely with the psychologist Henry Wallon, a well-know Communist. Several foreigners had found work in the laboratory and the employees were active in the science workers' union; some of them belonged to the Communist Party. Although the professors of the medical and legal faculties were mostly conservative, often strict Catholics, among the natural scientists there were a number of militant Communists, beginning with the "old guard," the famous physicists Madame Curie, J. Perrin, Paul Langevin and the biologist M. Prenant down to the most gifted of the younger scientists such as Frederic Joliot and Jacques Solomon. Frederic Joliot-Curie, who during the Popular Front government had been given responsibility for science, reorganized the research programs, which were becoming obsolescent, hired young administrators and promoted the development of all areas of scientific work. Thanks to the new opportunities, Pieron was able to offer Jascha a position as technical assistant in his laboratory, with a salary equivalent to two hundred marks per month. Jascha worked for the greater part of his time in Professor Pieron's laboratory. He received all the equipment and money that he needed to carry out his own research in the evenings and on Saturdays. I became an unpaid volunteer at the wine laboratory of the Institut National Agronomique, a specialized agricultural post-secondary school and also earned about fifty marks a month with translations and writing articles. We were able to work at our professions and had enough money to live on. Compared to most émigrés, we had it really good. Under the Popular Front government life became easier. There now was a social security system, inadequate but at least functional and, something then unknown in France, paid vacations. Public housing was being constructed – we were very optimistic.

We rented an apartment in the Latin Quarter, with heating, bathroom and kitchen - a mini-apartment without an entryway, about twenty square meters in size and we bought kitchen furniture and planks, which we painted blue. We were able to bring everything else from Germany. Although we could not have official contacts to the German organization, because we were still traveling to Berlin and carrying out the most varied assignments, there were still a number of comrades who visited us. We were also good friends with the Austrian comrades. They came to see us often, to pour out their hearts or, for once, to enjoy a culinary, refined meal. Cooking was, for us, an experimental art and I copied elements of many national styles. Once when I was sick, a German relative offered to cook for us. After the first meal Jascha told her, in a friendly way, that she needn't trouble herself any longer, he could manage alone. When she was gone, he sat down on my bed and hugged me and said, "Teddybear, I love you with all my heart, but if your cooking was like Ruth's, we would fight every day." In later years, when our French guests praised my cuisine, he used to say: "Teddy's cooking is her political secret weapon."

In 1937 my parents-in-law visited us in Paris. My father-in-law had accepted our marriage and spoiled me in a nice way. "I was very much against your marriage," he said, "not only because of your Christian upbringing, but especially because I was afraid that Jascha would give up his studies to earn money for his family. But I can't object to the way you're managing things. You are supporting Jascha in his work and adjusting to circumstances. Besides, he's working at one of the best scientific institutes in the world. So I'm prepared to keep on helping you if you need it,"

My mother-in-law, on the other hand, was totally lacking in comprehension. I've often observed that Jewish mothers and housewives from middle-class circles had a limited horizon and, in contrast to their husbands, learned nothing from events. They understood nothing that was not connected with their households and their children. The first thing that Mama Segal said was "You've got to persuade Jascha to study medicine. What am I going to tell the people in Kaunas, when they ask me what my son does? A physiologist? That's not a Jewish profession!" People in Kaunas must not have known the roster of Nobel Prize winners in physiology.

Strange as it may seem, my mother-in-law had experienced the Russian Revolution and the upheavals in Germany in a personal way and it had all rushed past her like a noise that she didn't hear.

We urged my father-in-law to sell his business in Lithuania and to retire in the South of France. But he and his wife strictly refused to discuss the dangerous situation on the borders of Germany. No-one in the family was thinking about retirement and they felt comfortable in Kaunas. No, they were definitely not moving to France.

My father-in-law died in May 1941, a few weeks before Lithuania was occupied by Hitler's army. His wife, his daughter, her husband and child and more than sixty relatives were murdered bestially in the first months of the Fascist occupation.

Marga

Fritz, Gerda's husband and
Marga's father.

It was not only my mother-in-law in Lithuania who failed to grasp the seriousness of the situation. My German family kept on sticking its head in the sand and trying to see nothing at all. Fritz Freudenthal died in 1936 of a kidney disease that he had contracted as a young volunteer in the first World War. My sister took care of him for many months and with the help of other doctors she succeeded in concealing the hopelessness of his situation from him. She also knew how to conceal from him all the humiliating administrative measures which now were also being imposed on German-Jewish combat veterans. Quite a few patients, who were actually not allowed to consult him, came to him privately.

My sister, after the death of her husband, decorated an elegant apartment for herself in Grunewald, had a tutor for her nine year old daughter Marga, improved her summer house on Sieten Lake and rejected any discussion of emigration. She couldn't give up her assets, she had a secure existence in Berlin.

Kurt Freudenthal, however, had continued to expand his illegal dental practice in Paris. He was doing well, financially and so he

Kurt Freudenthal, brother of Lilli's sister Gerda's deceased husband Fritz.

invited my sister to send, at least, her daughter Marga to Switzerland or to France: he would bear all the expenses for his niece. My sister rejected this suggestion too, supported in her life-threatening myopia by relatives and acquaintances.

In 1937 my brother emigrated to America with the help of a sponsorship. He had won it with his charm, in the most literal sense of the word. The only things he could take with him were a movie camera, several still cameras, a typewriter and a couple of elegant suits. One of his grieving girlfriends, who had travelled with him to Paris, sat in our apartment after his departure, seeking consolation. Since she was pretty and nice, Jascha was not reluctant to provide it.

Then came the 29th of September 1938. At Munich, France and England gave Hitler their agreement to the occupation of the Sudetenland. The Sudeten had belonged to the old Austria; at the foundation of Czechoslovakia it had been merged with Bohemia. During the war in Spain the Allies had given the Fascist troops a free hand. The Munich agreement, however, openly sanctioned the Nazi demands for power.

Six weeks later, on November 9, 1938, the Nazis organized the first comprehensive pogrom against the Jews. They no longer feared public opinion in the democratic countries. In the so-called "Night of Broken Glass" (Kristallnacht). almost three hundred synagogues and more than seven thousand Jewish businesses were destroyed, looted and burned out by the SS, the Storm

Troopers and the mob. Old people were beaten to the ground and thousands of Jewish men were dragged off to concentration camps.

Now my family, including my sister, finally understood. She was fortunately in possession of a visitor's visa to the USA. However, she could not leave her eleven year old daughter in Berlin. Max Maennlein, who later became my sister's second husband, brought the child to Munich. There a part of the Catholic population was outraged at the cruelty of the Jewish persecution. Marga was safe for the time being with one of Maennlein's aunts. We were informed that the girl was on her way to Paris. Christian friends had bought a sleeping car ticket for her. On the scheduled evening Max Maennlein went with Marga to the train station; he gave the sleeping car conductor the child's identity card bearing the stamp "Jew", together with a fifty mark note, remarking that the child had no visa, but would be met by her relatives in Paris.

"You must be looking for the little lady," said the conductor to Jasha, as he walked along the sleeping car corridor with a searching look. "She's happy and contented. No problems at the border. It's quite simple." With that he lifted up a stack of passports and pulled out the compromising identity card with the red stamp. "It got lost under all the bureaucratic rubbish," he said smiling.

Marga quickly adjusted to Paris. After just four days she was going by herself on the Metro and the bus to visit her uncle Kurt, who was paying all her expenses, but had no time for her even on weekends. During the first days we had entrusted her to one of our oldest friends, an Austrian comrade who spoke an undiluted Viennese dialect. It was the only time that Marga complained about one of our friends. "I really can't understand him, he speaks Chinese!" she said.

We got Marga settled into a children's home run by German Social Democrats and enrolled her at once in a French school and she was happy and satisfied. With her black hair and dark eyes, in a very delicate face, she looked completely French. She quickly learned how to alter her clothes, or got Uncle Kurt to buy new ones for her, so that soon one couldn't tell her from the little Parisiennes. Like all the other German émigré children, she liked going to the French school and quickly got over the language barrier. We grownups had a hard time explaining this phenomenon. To us, the French schools looked like prisons: dark, crowded classrooms, no sports, classes all morning and all afternoon, constant examinations and memorization followed by more memorization.

Still, the children found the school interesting and pleasant. They almost always had good relationships with the teachers, both male and female, who were mostly married and had children themselves. The teachers' union in France was one of the most progressive of all the trade unions; it even had anarchist tendencies.

On September 3, 1939, the first day of the war between France and Germany, Marga's Uncle Kurt, like all the other German emigrants, regardless of whether they had German citizenship or were stateless, was interned and his bank account was impounded. Fortunately we had moved to a two room apartment in August so that we could take Marga to live with us. She was enrolled in a school in our quarter of Paris and got along well in the new class. But after about three weeks she came home in tears and told us that that morning a social worker had reviewed the files of all the children. When she got to Marga's file, she said, in a rather unfriendly tone: "What are you doing here? You're a German; you belong in Germany, not here. Where are your parents?"

Marga answered hesitantly, that her mother had emigrated to America. "We'll have to take a very close look at this case. I'll deal with it in the morning," said the lady. Jascha sat down at once and wrote her a strong letter. He asked her whether, as a social worker, she occasionally read newspapers, in which she might be able to learn something about the situation in Nazi Germany and that she must have heard something, even in France, about the persecution of Jews. He was responsible for the child and placed himself at the disposition of the social worker.

We could see clearly that the self-confident, light-hearted, carefree Marga was deeply troubled. She wept bitterly and was afraid of being taken out of the school. Finally she accepted the letter. That afternoon she came back looking radiant. "The social worker smiled when she read the letter. Then she asked me if I liked staying with you and when I said yes, she nodded her head and said, I should stay with my aunt and my uncle, they would certainly take good care of me, I'm safe with you."

Unfortunately things did not remain as safe as they appeared, in September of 1939. When in May 1940 German troops marched from Belgium and Holland into France and Paris was terrified by the first air raid alarms, Marga's fear reappeared. Fortunately, we were able to place her, thanks to her uncle's contacts, in a Jewish children's home and a short time later the children, including her, were evacuated to the South, into the Massif Central, in the zone which was not occupied by the Germans. Since her mother was in the USA, she got on the emigration list and was able, in September of 1941, to go there by way of Portugal. As a grown woman, Marga likes to remember her time in France and after many years she still visits our friends in Paris.

During the era of the Popular Front in France, the political émigrés were able to breathe freely for the first time. The defense of Spain, the courage and enthusiasm of all those who fought in the International Brigades, gave us grounds for hope that the forces of democracy would prevail over Fascism after all. But under pressure from the Right and the French military, the Social Democratic Premier, Leon Blum, refused to deliver arms to the legally constituted Spanish Republic.

Together with the British he suggested a non-intervention pact, according to which all foreign troops would be withdrawn from Spain. The Soviet Union was compelled to sign this agreement and the military advisers and the International Brigades left Spanish territory, while Hitler and Mussolini sent their air force squadrons from Italy to Franco's aid, which decided the war in his favor.

The Communist Party of France did all it could to help the Spanish Republic. Comrades left their well-paid jobs to transport supplies across the Pyrenees, on trucks, on carts and on their backs. When the International Brigades were dissolved and the first Spaniards began fleeing into France, there was a real people's movement to keep the refugees out of the clutches of the authorities. The government interned them in an inhuman way in so-called reception camps. To be sure, no one in Gurs or Argeles was beaten or tortured, but the material and hygienic conditions there were significantly worse than in normal French prisons. Feuchtwanger's masterly characterization of the moral situation of those who were interned later on, in his book "The Devil in France", applies just as well to the members of the International Brigade.

After the Munich Agreement the situation of refugees from Germany also became much more insecure. To get a visa one had to have good contacts or a lot of money, even if one were a German Jew coming from a concentration camp. Political refugees could no longer obtain residence permits. Some comrades were expelled from the country or even dumped on the Belgian or Swiss frontiers.

Fortunately, the "Devil in France" was not only slovenly but often venal and the French Left was helpful.

The Communist, Social Democratic and Radical Socialist members of the Chamber of Deputies arranged residence permits for refugees, even when they officially had already been expelled from France.

One of our friends used to say, "An 'interdiction de sejour' an order of expulsion from France, bearing an extension stamp of the Prefecture of Police, is the best paper that a denaturalized German Jew can have – the police will always renew it!"

The French Right became increasingly aggressive in reaction to the victories of the Popular Front and the pro-Fascist elements in the army and the government were trying to win the upper hand. More than a thousand officers had formed a secret organization called the "Cagoule" – "the Hood" – along the lines of the Ku Klux Klan. They committed murders and attempted to stage a "coup d'état." Still, we felt ourselves to be generally safe from Fascism in republican France during 1938-39.

The crisis, when it came, was fully unexpected: the non-aggression pact between the Soviet Union and Hitler's Germany on August 24, 1939. At breakfast time we still believed that it was a slander campaign by the right-wing press, but by midday there could no longer be any doubt. My colleagues at the viticulture laboratory, who were already anti-Soviet, simply shrugged their shoulders, as if they had always known it would happen. In my husband's laboratory, on the other hand, all hell broke loose. Liberals and democrats demanded that he take a stand, as if he were responsible for what had happened. The comrades crept away into the most obscure corners of the Collège de France – they were completely helpless.

On the same evening our closest friends came to us, among them Lucie, a political comrade, who worked for the press agency of the Spanish Republic. Her husband was a member of the International Brigades who was now missing. She was politically the most experienced of all of us. We tried to analyze the situation, but we could not explain why the Soviet Union, precisely in August 1939, when Hitler was openly preparing to attack Poland, would, through this pact, apparently give him a free hand. After we had disputed the issue for some time, Lucie suddenly spoke and calmly said: "Let's think this thing through for once. What's the real situation? Since 1937 Hitler has steadily increased his expansionist demands. Austria, the Sudeten area, Czechoslovakia and now Poland. Every time, he promised that it was his final territorial demand. The Allies stood by calmly and looked on. When the Soviet Union offered to confront Hitler jointly with England and France, in Spain and during the attack on Czechoslovakia, they quickly reached an agreement with Hitler. Why? Because they wanted to see Hitler expand eastwards. They wanted him to have the largest staging area possible, when he was ready to make war on the Soviet Union. Hitler is the predatory beast that one feeds so that it will attack one's opponent. And now what's happened? The well-fed lion lets itself be stroked by its intended victim and won't bite it. But if Hitler has made a deal with the victim he was supposed to attack, then they won't allow him to grab any more territory. Now, suddenly, they're afraid of him; now there's going to be war. And here in France the war will begin by persecuting the Communists under the excuse that they're making common cause with Germany."

And that was what happened. On September 1, 1939, when German troops attacked Poland, France remembered its alliances with Czechoslovakia and Poland. The government proclaimed a general mobilization and on September 3 England and immediately afterwards France, officially declared war on Germany.

In fact, troops were sent to the French border in Alsace and Lorraine where they took up positions. Poorly equipped, without adequate air cover, commanded in large part by officers who, like their commanding general Weygand, belonged to the Catholic, anti- Republican reaction and were more afraid of a new popular movement than of the Germans, the war of position began. Both sides sent out occasional patrols and from time to time shots were exchanged and Hitler gained the time he needed to bring his war machine up to speed. Not a single bomb fell on the arms factories on the Ruhr and the Rhine. Of one thousand six hundred English airplanes that were sent to France, only eight hundred were fit for combat.

A joke made the rounds of Paris: the English send a squadron of airplanes to the Ruhr to throw out leaflets urging the Germans to stop the war. The squadron comes back, minus one pilot. Hours go by. In the grey dawn, after he's been reported missing, he lands. Everybody pounces on him: what's wrong? Did you have an accident? "What accident," he says, surprised.
'It took a while to put all those leaflets in the mailboxes."

This war soon got the name "la drôle de guerre" – the funny war.

Although the government did not take the war seriously, it compensated for this deficit by the earnestness with which it pursued its fight against the anti-Fascists and especially the Communists. The Communist deputies declared their readiness to defend democracy and the independence of the country. The Communist Party urged all its members who were called to the colors to do their utmost to defend France. Despite this, the Communists were branded by the government and the bourgeois press as traitors.

On September 29 the Communist Party of France was prohibited and the immunity of its parliamentary deputies was revoked. A number of well-known German and foreign Communists had already been arrested in the last days of August under the pretext that they constituted a fifth column, Women who were thought suspect were sent to the Rieucros camp, near Mende in the South of France. Our German women comrades were also imprisoned there along with many foreign women. I know of no case in which members of a fifth column were actually arrested, nor of German women who consorted with French army officers being arrested either.

Starting with the day of mobilization there were raids every day in the Latin Quarter where we lived. Jascha and I only needed to walk along the Boulevard Saint Michel, for a police officer to stop us and ask for our papers. Although I had bought all my dresses in Germany and looked quite German with my flat heels and without a hat and although my identity card stated that I had been born in Berlin, my papers were always returned to me without further formalities. The officer often added, "Please excuse me, Madame." Jascha's identity card, on the other hand, was studied from beginning to end in the most precise way and he constantly had to answer curious and unfriendly questions. One evening I blew up and snapped at the officer, quite rudely: "Can you please tell me, why you constantly harass my husband, a Lithuanian born in Saint Petersburg and a French government employee, while you never seriously inspect me, a born German?"

"Madame," the officer replied, "if you don't want your husband to be stopped and checked by every cop he runs across, then don't let him run around with this leather jacket. With his blond hair and the glasses and this jacket, he looks like the image of a Russian commissar. You might be aware of our directives: not a word in them about German women!"

And indeed, after I had forced the reluctant Jascha to hang up the leather jacket, we were able to stroll the boulevards in the evening undisturbed.

On September 3 came the official decree, according to which all men born in Austria and Germany between the ages of seventeen and fifty-six had to report to the authorities. They were interned as enemy aliens. No distinction was made between those who were stateless and Austrian or German. Thousands of children of Polish parents, who had been born in Germany, had never had German nationality, or it had been revoked on racial and political grounds after 1933. Since the reactionary Polish government did not want to issue passports to them, they were registered in France as stateless and were officially under the protection of the League of Nations. That did not in the least hinder the authorities from arresting them as Germans together with German Nazis. Many of the men were taken to the Orleans area where they were held provisionally at an abandoned factory site with inadequate sanitary conditions. During the first weeks they got neither mail nor packages, although winter had begun in the meantime. Their wives were informed that they were not permitted to leave the town they lived in, no matter if they were registered emigrants or women from the German Reich with regular German passports. The money and possessions of all those interned were confiscated as enemy assets.

Once again, we were in a privileged situation. Jascha had his position at the Collège de France.

To be sure we still had our niece Marga with us, but Romanian relatives were providing some financial support. So it was no wonder, that the wives of our comrades came to us with their troubles, for one thing, because we had a neutral, non-compromising address. An Austrian comrade called our apartment the "Segal Committee".

Jascha, after consulting his French colleagues and comrades, volunteered for the French army. After only two weeks he got a summons. He was presented with a contract for a five year enlistment in the Foreign Legion. When he stated that he wanted to fight for France against Hitler and would not dream of firing on the natives in the French colonies. The officer became wild with rage. Jascha refused to sign and nothing happened.

Recruiting for the Foreign Legion also took place in the internment camps. Our "Segal Committee" became active here. I shoved many cakes into my very primitive oven. Sometimes they didn't get done all the way through, sometimes they were slightly burned, but every single one had a message in it with guidelines and important information for the men.

There were, to be sure, voices in France, primarily among the leftist parliamentarians in the group surrounding Pierre Cot, who were angry at the fact that Hitler's victims were the first to be locked up, while the fifth column continued to do its dirty work. But the newspapers published almost nothing about this. The

"Epoque" was an exception. Its publisher, de Kerillis, a genuine French nationalist, had demanded in the first days of the war, that Germany had to be defeated. After a consultation with some of the Austrian women comrades I requested an interview with de Kerillis.

I am actually not receptive to the charm of the Latin nations and still less to what is called a handsome man. Still, even I, simply as a woman, was impressed by this slender, athletic man with the radiant eyes. A knight without fear and without reproach, perhaps the last knight in France!

We had put together a dossier about conditions in the camps, about the fathers of French children, about members of the Legion of Honor, men who had done their military service in France and were now sitting in the camp. We compared this group to those who had been released as special cases, for the most part German nationals who were married to French women. "Do you know," de Kerillis interrupted me, "who was the first one to be released? The porter at the Brown House. (This propaganda center of Hitler's Reich only employed fanatical Nazis.) The gentlemen of the Fifth Column are very often married to French women. I really have no sympathy for the Germans, but the treatment of those who are being persecuted by Hitler mocks every description."

"If you will allow me, I'd like to add a small personal experience to my report," I said and I told him about Kurt Freudenthal, the circumstances under which he had had to leave Germany and whom he had treated in his dental practice. I described his German dental assistant, who had a German passport and of course had often traveled to Germany and said that Kurt had asked me to bring her a letter for one of his former patients. I told him about my astonishment, when I entered the lady's hotel room and saw the uniform jacket of an officer in the French air force hanging there. The officer was just enjoying his breakfast and made no effort to conceal his relationship to the blonde German beauty.

"I give you my word of honor," replied de Kerillis, shaking his head, "that I will do everything to help the victims of German Fascism and to ensure that the real enemies are imprisoned."

De Kerillis kept his promise. He advised me to give the report to a famous American journalist, Knickerbocker, who was returning to New York in the next few days. I wasn't able to speak to Knickerbocker personally, but it reached him. He used it to mobilize New York Jews to help the internees in France.

On November 30, 1939, the Soviet Union attacked the Finnish Mannerheim-Line, at that time the most modern defense line, only 32 kilometers north of Leningrad. Everyone knew, that it was impossible for little Finland to construct such an expensive line of fortifications, armed with the most modern defensive weapons, without the help of powerful friends. And in fact, as we later learned, the Mannerheim-Line had been built by England and later modernized by Nazi Germany. Also, it was known that Mannerheim had very close connections to the German General Staff.

The French press almost forgot that France and Germany were at war. Headlines in the newspapers pilloried the "Attack by the Soviet Union". Unfortunately this propaganda was successful with many middle-class democrats. This time the anti-communist smear campaign had an even greater effect. Even we were confused and, like our friends, we sought an explanation. However, it soon became clear to us that the uproar about events in Finland was intended as a diversion from the "funny war" and the sham maneuvers of the General Staff. At the end of January 1940 France began to equip an expeditionary force for Finland.

It was provided with the most modern weapons, winter clothing and special winter equipment. This in turn caused outrage among the French, because they knew that the soldiers of the twenty divisions that were stationed on the French-German frontier, behind the famous Maginot Line, were lacking the most necessary supplies. A doctor who was a friend of ours told us that ninety per cent of all the war wounded in the winter of 1939/40 were suffering from pneumonia or frostbite.

We first began to understand the necessity of the Finnish-Russian conflict in 1941, as Leningrad was under siege and the city was able to resist Hitler's troops for more than two years. If the Germans had been able to occupy the Mannerheim-Line, then heroic Leningrad would have fallen after a few days. The well-equipped expeditionary forces of the French and English came too late. The line of fortifications, considered insurmountable, fell in March. On April 9, 1940 German troops occupied Norway. The invasion of Holland and Belgium followed at the beginning of May, enabling the Fascist Wehrmacht to bypass the Maginot Line. Within fourteen days Belgium and Holland were overrun, while the English offered no resistance from the air. German bombers, meanwhile, were already attacking cities in northern France.

Once again our political activity consisted in forwarding letters, packing suitcases and packages, making our address available as a collection point for those wives who had been transported by the French police to one place or another and who did not know how to locate their husbands.

CHAPTER VII

Tour de France

"These defenseless rivers of humanity were frequently attacked by German dive bombers."

And then came blow after blow. The French army held out for three days in the Ardennes; on May 15 Sedan was lost. The French army retreated southwards. Military columns and fleeing civilians strove to reach the Seine, hoping that the enemy could be stopped there. The German Luftwaffe bombarded military columns and fleeing civilians. On June 5 the decisive battle for France was fought in Normandy. One hundred German divisions were engaged. The French supreme commander, General Weygand, stated: "To save the army, we must preserve order," but in reality he organized the defeat. In the ministries the flight from Paris was prepared.

During the first days of June Jascha tried once again to enlist, but there was no one at the recruiting station to take his enlistment. On June 9 the Germans broke through the last front at Rouen and marched on Paris. On June 10 the ministries began to evacuate their employees and the general population was encouraged to leave Paris. The chaos of this exodus was indescribable. There were no plans for an evacuation. Jascha turned to his department for guidance. The managers were all gone; he was ordered to go to a safe place of his own choosing and as far as possible to take the most valuable laboratory equipment with him, so that it wouldn't fall into the hands of the Germans.

All public transport, except the Metro, had been requisitioned; the trains were occupied by the army. The train stations were all under smoke screens, which made the confusion worse.

The Parisians fled their city, in old cars and new cars, some of them models from before the first world war and in horse-drawn wagons, in trucks, with carts, with pushcarts, with baby buggies, we even saw a group of people in a hearse, seated on a coffin. All the roads were open to civilians, so that they got among the military formations and brought them to a halt. These defenseless rivers of humanity were frequently attacked by German dive bombers using the presence

Photo of French civilians escaping the Nazi invasion.

of the military as an excuse. There has never been even an approximate accounting of the numbers of dead and wounded.

Although we still didn't grasp that this was the end, although we still believed that the Hitler troops would be stopped at the Loire, we did understand this much: we needed to prepare ourselves for a long period of rather unpleasant conditions. We bought ourselves a rubber mattress and a small tent, under which we often camped in the time that followed. We called it our "snail shell". We took windbreakers, track suits, short pants, bandages, liquid soap, canned foods, rice and a little petrol cooker which we used during our involuntary "Tour de France" to prepare our meals.

And so, on June 12, we left Paris on two bicycles and melded into the eight million civilians and soldiers who now populated the roads of France.

The sun shone hot out of a deeply blue sky, the meadows were green and the wheat in the fields was already shining a bright yellow. Between the fields, the roads filled with cars, people in brightly colored summer clothes and the strangest looking baggage: a motley, indescribable picture.

About fifty kilometers south of Paris, at Fontainebleau, we ran into the first traffic jams. Army tanks, cannons, tanker trucks and columns of military trucks blocked the roads. The trucks were stuffed full of soldiers, often in their shirt sleeves and covered with a layer of dust as if they had been traveling for days through the desert. Most of them looked tired, indifferent and completely unmilitary. Often there were no officers to be seen.

With our bicycles we were able to wind our way between the cars and military vehicles. In places where the road was totally blocked, we dismounted and shoved the bikes along the shoulder of the road or across the fields. We often encountered single cars with officers, cut off from their troops by civilian vehicles. Quite a few civilians shed their inhibitions and told the officers to their faces that they were cowards who had plunged France into war and were now running away. The soldiers also came in for their share of abuse. Several times, when we had stopped at a roadside café to have something to drink and study our simple automobile roadmaps of France, to figure out the best route, we were approached by a non-commissioned officer or a driver, asking for a look at the map. When the soldiers were ordered to withdraw, they had not been issued any maps whatever and thus often had no idea where they were. There were, of course, formations which moved in good order led by their officers. The civilians treated these units with respect.

When we left Paris I was a little afraid that as foreigners we would be suspected of espionage. After all, my papers stated clearly, "Born in Berlin". But we quickly saw that no controls were possible in this chaos. Many people thought Jascha was an Englishman because of his light blond hair, narrow face and slender build and they berated him accordingly.

People already knew that the British had no choice but to save the remainder of their army by retreating by boat to England. When we passed a car on the left, against traffic regulations, the driver would yell: "We're not in England! We drive on the right here! Go back to your island, Tommy!"

On the second day we approached the Loire. This broad river forms a natural border between northern and southern France. Here we met troops from Alsace streaming from east to west. Everywhere, the soldiers told the same story. They hadn't fired a shot: suddenly the Germans were there and their officers had disappeared. The situation got more and more desperate. Grocery stores were already almost empty, there were long lines in front of the bakeries and even water was becoming scarce. The lines of cars that had run out of gas kept getting longer. Soldiers coming from the south, from the Orleans area, reported that many bridges over the Loire had been bombed and that the troops were sitting in a trap. More and more one heard people saying: "If only it were over! Why don't they just stop? We've been sold out! Our men should come home, not play the fool with the military."

The forces of reaction had accomplished their aim: people saw themselves facing a horrible ending. They were psychologically prepared for surrender.

We kept on moving southwards. The front was about one hundred kilometers behind us: the German tank columns advanced about eighty kilometers a day and we had to put at least that much distance behind us on our overloaded bicycles, in order not to be overrun.

On the second evening we found ourselves near Nevers, an important crossing point on the Loire, about two hundred and twenty kilometers south of Paris. Exhausted, we found an empty courtyard and lay down in our tent and slept like the dead. Early the next morning, three soldiers woke us. "Well, look at the love-birds," the oldest of the three said, laughing good naturedly. "You're sleeping here like babes and missing the whole fire-works." To our astonished questions they answered: "The Germans bombed Nevers last night, you need to get across the Loire. We've got room in our truck, we can take you part of the way."

I quickly fixed some porridge on our gas cooker and the soldiers ate it with enthusiasm. A Frenchman has to be very hungry indeed to eat porridge. Half an hour later we were in the convoy that was about to cross the bridge at Nevers. The roar of motors: two German dive bombers were swooping over the bridge at about two hundred meters altitude. A flash and a loud explosion. The pilots flew around once again and then away. Jascha pointed to two small cannons standing on the opposite shore.

"Vintage 1914." he said, quite calmly. "There won't be a defense line behind the Loire, either."

What to do? One thing was clear: this leaderless army without modern weapons or morale appeared to be vanquished, even if isolated groups had not given up. As someone. I don't know who, put it so well: it was not a defeat but a coup d'état, abetted by organized chaos.

We made a quick decision to reach the Rieucros camp near Mende in southern France in order to arrange some kind of aid to the women comrades interned there, who were now endangered.

Our papers were good, we were mobile thanks to our bicycles and we even had funds at our disposal. For a long time we had been managing a large sum belonging to my father in-law. In normal times, of course, we would never have touched it. Now we agreed at once that we could use the money for ourselves and for the victims of Hitler's terror.

People have often asked us why, despite war, illegality and all the difficulties, we never regarded our situation as tragic and why, in many situations, we acted with a certain rashness and lack of forethought. What's certain is that we always agreed on what we wanted to do and in our opinion had to do. That gave us courage and confidence. We felt that we could not simply stand by and watch what was happening. And so without long discussions, we decided, on that July 14th, while we watching the collapse at the Loire and the news came through that Paris had been occupied, that we were going to do everything we could to overcome all the obstacles and get to the South.

Late in the evening, totally exhausted, we reached Vichy, a fashionable spa that made the impression of an encampment during the wars of the Turks. Officers, soldiers, military police and civilian police – the rearguard of the French army appeared to be assembled here. Men in uniform were running around in utter confusion. Private autos were being stopped outside the city – the general staff of the army was in Vichy. Still, nobody paid any attention to two cyclists with their packs. To be sure, a guard was posted before the biggest hotel on the main street, but he stared proudly over the heads of us mere civilians.

One of my Romanian relatives had given me a letter of reference to a Romanian lady, who ran a very elegant lingerie shop on the main street of Vichy. We found the shop and the lady, but she was already putting up six Romanians in her storerooms.

"The only thing I can offer you," she said, with Romanian hospitality, "is a place in my show window. I'll put a screen in front of your bed." Any place was welcome, provided we could stretch out on our rubber mattresses. And so it happened that we spent the night of June 14 to 15 surrounded by frilly ladies' underwear in a shop window, thirty meters from the headquarters of the French general staff. We slept like children and didn't notice that the screen fell down during the night. In the morning we lay in a close embrace amongst the pink silk nightdresses in the show window. There was so much excitement and general confusion that no one noticed anything.

In the next four days we covered the nearly three hundred kilometers to Mende. The route took us across the Massif Central, a considerable mountain range. The stream of refugees had begun to split up and several times, on a steeply ascending highway, we were able to soften the heart of a passing military truck driver, who would then give us a lift.

On June 18, 1940, the day on which France first offered a cease-fire, we reached Mende, in the Departement Lozere. Mende is a picturesque little town in the Cevennes, a chain of mountains in the South of France. We took a room in the only hotel in town and quickly learned that the police inspector in charge of the women's camp of Rieucros was also staying there. We applied to him for a permit to visit our "Cousin Lucie". This alleged kinship made it possible for us to officially give assistance to this very compromised comrade and her four year old daughter.

The inspector explained to us courteously: "I am terribly sorry, but just six hours ago I received express orders from Vichy to let no one into the camp and no one out of it. As you are probably aware, all the main roads have been closed since early this morning. No one is allowed to leave the Department."

Fortunately comrade Vera Trail was also living in the hotel. She had been interned in the camp for three months and had made friends with Lucie during that time. Vera came from a white Russian family but she had frequently demonstrated her support for the

Soviet Union. Her husband, an Englishman, had been a member of the International Brigade in Spain, as well as a number of her Russian émigré friends. Since she had English nationality, she was allowed to leave the camp. She was not, however, allowed to leave Mende.

"Don't worry about the cops," she said in her flawless French. "things in the camp are completely disorganized; with a little nerve you can get in." She went with me to buy important groceries and lent me a bag in which we placed a fresh head of lettuce, making sure it was visible and off I went. The camp consisted of a number of wooden barracks, surrounded by a barbed wire fence. There were only two strands and I only had to hold one up and the other down and step through: it was child's play. The streetwalkers who had been locked up here with the political women used this way out of the camp when they were going to meet the off-duty soldiers. Sometimes I stumbled over one of these couples in the surrounding woods.

The gate to the camp, however, also stood wide open. I went to the office, showed the staff my fresh lettuce and explained that I wanted to give it to my Cousin Lucie today: tomorrow it would be spoiled.

Nobody asked for my papers. After some hesitation I was warned not to stay more than ten minutes, which I promised not to do. Lucie was shocked when she saw me. Her first question was "For God's sake, did they find out that you're a German?" I explained the military situation and asked her to tell the German comrade Edith Freund that we were here. We made an appointment for the following day, during that time sacred to all Frenchmen, the lunch break. We were to meet at the barbed wire. After that, we met every day. Sometimes I sneaked through the wire to bring something into the camp. Sometimes Lucie had a chat with Jascha across the fence. The athletic Edith Freund, on the other hand, always cleared the wire in a single bound, and we would spend time together in the open.

Because we were unable, at the moment, to do anything more to help, we decided to take our bicycles and explore the Department and look for possible ways of getting out of Mende. I must admit that we enjoyed these tours through the canyons of the Tarn river and across the Cevennes. To be sure, we worried about the situation of our friends, but we were still not aware of the full extent of the tragedy of the defeat. Camping out under the stars, searching for water in this arid landscape, starting a fire to cook something: all that was like an adventure. Jascha and I were very much in love.

When we got back to Mende the ceasefire had been agreed on in the forest of Compiegne. The eighty-four year old Marshal Petain, known for his pro-Fascist attitude, signed in the name of the French general staff and assumed the power to govern in the unoccupied part of France, the so-called "Free Zone". More than half of the country, northern France down to the Loire and the Atlantic coast down to the Spanish border, remained under German military occupation and under the administration of Hitler's generals.

At the same time, General de Gaulle, who had gone to London with the British and some nationalist Frenchmen, had formed a government in exile of "Free France". At the end of June, Radio London was already broadcasting his proclamation in which he refused to recognize the surrender. He and a number of other officers would continue the war side by side with England. The newspapers had published a passage of the ceasefire agreement, according to which all German emigrants whose names were supplied to the French authorities by the German occupiers, had to be handed over to them. This applied to all active anti-Fascists, especially the members of the International Brigades from the war in Spain and many known Communists. It could be assumed that the most active comrades from Rieucros would be on such a list. We urgently needed to get in contact with Edith Freund. The ban on visitors to the camp had been lifted, so we went to the inspector and asked for a visitor's pass. He smiled and said, "Why do you need a pass? You visited your cousin every day last week anyway."

"We don't want you to have problems," was my answer, which he acknowledged with "You are most considerate, Madame."

The plan we laid out for Edith was intended primarily to help the most endangered comrades. Within five to fifteen kilometers of Mende there were a number of bus lines offering trips to Marseilles, where they could go underground. We had indicated on a map the routes to take to reach the bus stations and we wanted to give each of the comrades several hundred francs, out of my father-in-law's funds.

After three days we got an answer to our offer: "No, we can't accept your suggestion, we don't want to separate; as long as we stay together we're strong."

But since you're Lithuanians and Lithuania is being incorporated into the Soviet Union on August 1, we ask you to contact the Soviet consulate and to hand over a list of those comrades who are especially at risk, so that their release from the camp can be arranged." Lucie, whose mother was living in Moscow with Andor Gabor, an important Hungarian author and a leading comrade, asked us to ask the Soviet consul to forward news about her to her mother.

The consulate was in Vichy with the newly-formed Petain government. Again we were in luck. Jascha had after all been working for an institute that was directly under the Ministry of Education. So we applied again to the police for a "Laissez Passer", a travel permit, so that Jascha could report for work at his institute. There was a long discussion at the police station. "How are you going to get there? There's no public transport. On bicycles, over the mountains? Where will you find shelter?" Finally, after giving us the permit, the officer explained that in principle no foreigners were allowed to enter Vichy. The inspector of the camp at Rieucros, who was sitting in the room, commented: "If I know them, they'll get through all the blockades!"

And we did. On July 25 we were rolling through the streets of Vichy, which was full of military men in elegant uniforms. There were furniture trucks parked everywhere because all the big hotels were being remodeled as ministries and administrative buildings.

We took shelter in a stable that was serving as a refugee center, where we got our own horse stall with straw on the floor. We weren't allowed to camp outdoors; the first decrees of the Petain government did not apply to the military or to the return of the refugees to their homes, but to the Christian morality of the population.

And so it was not only forbidden to pitch a tent outdoors, but also to go swimming outdoors and women were not allowed to wear shorts. The police who had stopped us on our way to Vichy had taken exception only to my short pants and naked legs.

The Soviet consulate was easy to find and the consul received us very cordially. He showed a lot of sympathy for the situation of the German comrades in Rieucros, but he was not able to do anything. All matters pertaining to visas had to be resolved in Paris, to which he had no direct connection. If we could manage to get to Paris, then everything would be taken care of, including our own situation, since we were now citizens of the Soviet Union and under its protection.

But how were we going to get back to Paris, inside the zone of German occupation? The line of demarcation was closed to civilians. Once again, we were helped by the fact that Jascha worked for the Ministry of Education. A Permanent Under-Secretary of the Ministry received us on the steps leading to the entrance to the hotel in which his Ministry had been housed. Jascha explained to him that he had not drawn his salary for two months and that he wanted to get back to his laboratory. The man responded in friendly fashion: "The authority you work for is located in Bordeaux now, so I can't give you travel orders for Paris. I can give you papers for Bordeaux. You're mobile, on your bicycles. Perhaps you can get back to Paris from Bordeaux. It's only a small detour for you." Our roadmap showed us that this "small detour" was about a thousand kilometers.

If we were to pass through the line of demarcation separating unoccupied from occupied France, with its military patrols, our travel orders had to be stamped by the military authorities. And in fact after three days we succeeded in penetrating the hall where the colonels sat, who with ceremonial expressions and much self-importance, decided on the applications that were brought before them. We spoke our piece to an elegant, good-looking, white-haired colonel. Suddenly he raised his head, looked at my husband as if to size him up and asked: "Excuse me, but am I correct in assuming that you are a Jew?"

"Yes indeed," answered Jascha.

"Well then, aren't you afraid of the Hitlerites?"

"No: we're neutral foreigners and enjoy protection."

"Beginning August 1 the Lithuanian consulate won't be able to protect you," warned the colonel.

"We've already made inquiries," said Jascha. "we're under the protection of the Soviet consulate."

"If you apply to the Soviet consulate, we will expel you from France."

That was an actual threat. Jascha and I spoke almost simultaneously. "So what?" said Jascha, while I said "Go right ahead!"

The colonel's mouth literally remained open. He took his stamp and banged it down on our paper, handed it to us and wished us "Bon voyage!"

And so we started on the next stage of our "Tour de France". We turned southwards, crossing the Massif Central with its breathtakingly beautiful valleys and towns and then we followed the lovely valley of the Dordogne. Crossing into the occupied area was completely unproblematic; the only objections raised by the gendarmes were directed at our bare legs.

In Bordeaux we were told that Jascha's institute had returned to Paris in the first days of August and that we would have to travel the last six hundred kilometers of our tour with our bicycles the next weeks. We saw little of the German occupation forces; the civilian population praised their orderliness and their calm.

To be sure, foodstuffs and textiles had quickly become scarce. For the first time we heard a new nickname for the Germans: *doryphores* – potato bugs – because they ate everything they came across.

CHAPTER VIII

1940 – 1943

Resistance – André

"This guy didn't register as a Jew? Lock him up!"

And then we were back in Paris, a grey sad city in October 1940, under German occupation. Our German and Austrian friends had almost all remained in the unoccupied zone. Starting in October we began to get letters asking us to close down people's apartments and if possible to ship their suitcases to Toulouse, Marseilles or Perigeux. And so, in the winter of 1940/41 one of our jobs was to move our comrades' suitcases through the streets of Paris on a hand truck and to hand them over to the baggage master at the Gare de Lyon.

By March 1941 the fifth month of my pregnancy was showing and people were sympathetic and helpful when we appeared with the hand truck.

The French leftist intellectuals and comrades of our acquaintance were generally dejected, confused and in fact passive. Just like us, they had believed that Hitler's army would encounter serious resistance. We learned more and more details that proved that Petain and the general staff had intentionally handed over not only ordinance depots, but the army itself, to the Germans. The Fascist government in France did not seem to consider it a national tragedy that more than one and a half million Frenchmen were in German prison camps. The nationalist Frenchmen and followers of General de Gaulle , whom we knew, had still not dared to come out of hiding. They felt themselves isolated and their main activity consisted in hiding escaped prisoners of war from the Germans.

By accident we made contact with a member of the Free German Youth, Roman Rubenstein and through him to the Party. An especially endangered German comrade, Fritz Buchmann, found shelter in our home and people wanted to use our new citizenship to establish contact with the Soviet Embassy. So we lined up with the other petitioners in front of the consulate. After several days we succeeded in getting through to a consular official. After we had filled out mountains of paper, it was explained to us that we would get a stamp in our passports, stating that we were registered with the Soviet consulate – more could not be done. On the other hand, they were prepared to accept our application for a visa to return to Lithuania.

The reaction to the list of German women, which we submitted together with other reports about endangered comrades, was much less friendly. Why was it our business to meddle in politics and intervene on behalf of Germans and stateless people? That could jeopardize the correct relations between Germany and the Soviet Union. This attitude first began to change, when the visa for our friend Lucie and her five year old daughter Madeleine, who was living with us, arrived from Moscow. As we later learned, the visa had been granted after a personal intervention by Georgi Dimitroff and her stepfather Andor Gabor. Within three days I had all the necessary documents in order to travel to the occupied zone, by rail this time, to hand little Madeleine over to her mother. And in fact the two traveled, together with some other women comrades, to the Soviet Union.

I used the journey to the unoccupied zone to make a side trip to Toulouse to visit some comrades. Naturally they overwhelmed me with errands to run in Paris. At that point, fortunately, the Brigade speciale, the branch of the French police into which the worst Fascists were later recruited for the purpose of fighting the Communists, had not yet been established. If it had, I definitely would have been caught.

This time I was asked to make contact with a leading comrade in Paris, who had found shelter with a Polish comrade. He was the holder of a Czechoslovak passport, under a false name. The real name of the "old man" as we later called him affectionately, was Paul Grasse. He had been a member of the Communist fraction of the Prussian state parliament. He was an authentic Berliner and a worker who had been active in the Party since his youth. He had been in a concentration camp for two years. After his release in 1936 he fled to Czechoslovakia. When Czechoslovakia was delivered to the Germans in 1938, the authorities had provided him and other comrades who were at risk with regulation Czechoslovak passports. Paul Grasse had escaped to France with his passport. He was over fifty at that point and it was no longer possible for him to learn to speak even passable French. But thanks to his practical intelligence and his wide experience of life, he had managed so far to survive all kinds of tricky situations. The "old man" not only had a solid Marxist education, he was also interested in social and cultural matters and he could empathize with the peculiarities of others. He got along well with the small Jewish artisans among whom he had, for a while, found refuge. Through him, we were officially initiated into illegal work. Later we maintained contact with him. We were the only ones who could solve certain urgent practical problems for him and we were bound to him by ties of genuine friendship.

Meanwhile our visas to return to Lithuania were ready at the Soviet consulate. The German authorities, though, refused to allow Jascha to travel through Germany. Once again we found ourselves sitting around at the consulate, often on behalf of other people who had entrusted their problems to us.

For example, two Russian emigrant women came to us with the following request: their husbands, who had fought in Spain, were interned at the La Vernet camp. A German commission had visited the camp and had made an offer both to them and to the Spaniards, to volunteer to work in Germany. If they did, they would be released at once and could live as free workers. We were requested to inquire at the Soviet consulate whether the Russian emigrants could accept this offer, or whether their return to the Soviet Union would be jeopardized. The consul didn't appear to understand the question. To our argument, that these men would be working voluntarily for a Fascist regime, the consul responded with a simple sentence: "If they can get out of the camp that way, we have no objection."

During the Great Patriotic War, Dick Pakrowski, who had gone to Germany by this route, passed on valuable information to us several times. It was through him that we first learned about the existence of the camp at Auschwitz; later he provided details about the production of remote controlled rockets by the Siemens firm. The brother of his wife, "Father Dimitri", helped to hide a number of Jews. In August 1941 he baptized our four week old son André according to the Orthodox rites. Father Dimitri's sister Tanya Pakrowski was the godmother. Because the priest was already on the blacklist, the baptism took place in our apartment.

According to Orthodox ritual, the godparents and we had to circle the baptismal font a number of times, while the bearded little priest held the cross aloft. The child was completely immersed. Out of respect for this quiet hero we played our part in the rite with suitable decorum and Father Dimitri was pleased to be able to issue at least one genuine baptismal certificate. A few months later he was arrested and sent, together with his loyal helper "Mother Maria", to Auschwitz. There he died the death of a martyr.

Our return to Lithuania became more and more problematic. It was clear that we had to prepare ourselves for a long stay in Paris. Romanian relatives, who had stayed in the free zone, let us use their comfortable and spacious four room apartment in a new building in a good neighborhood. The rent had been paid for a year in advance. The apartment had a rear entrance, so that it was possible to come in and go out without encountering the concierge, a much feared functionary in France. As a consequence, we seldom lived there alone. We gave shelter to as many as two women with three children. Romanian and German comrades, Poles, even the French, valued our middle-class quarters as a safe refuge. That the police took no notice of us, surpasses the miraculous. We only once had difficulties, when the wife of Phillip Holzmann, a German comrade, spent several weeks with us. Her child, whom she had with her, was seriously ill and cried all day long. When the neighbors complained and began asking questions, it was decided to send her and the child to the country.

Jascha was advised to seek work as a translator. He applied to a Mr. Max Gall, director of a private translation bureau and, as it turned out, a German residing in France. Gall had advertised on behalf of a central agency of the German Luftwaffe. And so the Lithuanian Jew Jacob Segalis became an interpreter for a German office. His experiences with the officers, who were mostly ardent Nazis, would fill a book by themselves – with the title "The Good Soldier Schweik In The German Luftwaffe In The Second World War".

Jascha's immediate boss, a qualified engineer named Diedelt, was as tall as he was stupid. He never caught on that Jascha followed all the regulations with the utmost precision, in order to block the transmission of important papers, or to reroute them counterproductively. To be sure, every evening Diedelt carefully locked up all the documents and stamps in the office safe; but when he went to lunch he left Jascha alone in the office with all the files. He never noticed that Jascha occasionally tried to get him out of the office. For example, Jascha would tell him that he had seen a special camera, or a special lens or some other hard to find technical apparatus somewhere in the city. "Have the car sent over; I need to go see this for myself," was the hoped for reaction.

Diedelt once invited us to a restaurant that was actually reserved for Germans. He wanted to give us a treat. The systematic confiscation of all raw materials by the German armies had led to a terrible food shortage. Even potatoes and noodles had become a delicacy. I was so undernourished that I could no longer tolerate a normal diet and I vomited up the nice pork cutlet and the pudding.

Jascha recognized as early as March 1941, that preparations for war in the east were being made. There were a series of unmistakable signs.

Other comrades, too, who had something to do with the German military authorities, brought us information about the remobilization of the German army and our French comrades were also convinced that something was afoot. Similar information trickled through from Holland and Belgium.

We were certainly not the only ones to communicate these facts to the Soviet Embassy, but as far as I know, everyone else got the same brush-off that we did. It simply seemed inconceivable that the Germans would wage war on two fronts. I will never forget how during the first days of June 1941 I sat in an advanced state of pregnancy in the office of the consul and wept. The visa for our return to Lithuania was still not in order.

I sobbed, "Now we won't be able to leave France before war starts." "That's ridiculous," said the consul, "by the time your baby is born, the papers will be straightened out and you can travel safe and sound to Lithuania."

The attack on the Soviet Union began fourteen days later. Our first reaction was that Jascha telephoned his office on June 23 and quit his job. The next day the German comrades told him that he must be crazy: he was given strict orders to go back to work. But how?

We hadn't considered Engineer Diedelt. On June 24 he came to our apartment. Jascha, he explained forcefully, was a Lithuanian and in two weeks Lithuania would be "liberated" and so there was no reason not to come back to work.

And so Jascha continued to work at the regional air command and I stayed in contact with the comrades right up to the day when I went into labor.

When our son André was six weeks old, all foreigners from the Baltic countries were ordered to register with the police. And then it happened: the policewoman at the precinct station looked at Jascha's alien identity card and said, " You're a Jew; why don't you have a Jew stamp? Your mother's name is Rebecca Schlimakowski and your name is Jacob. You have three days to report back here with your certificate of baptism, or be placed under arrest."

Jascha's arguments, that there were also Protestants named Rebecca and that he couldn't bring any such certificate, because he had been born in Leningrad, which was now in a war zone, so that there was no postal connection, left her entirely cold.

A week later Jascha was summoned to the Commissariat des Affaires Juives. That was the authority charged with the registration and arrest of Jews. Since he knew the French would want to inform his office, Jascha, to be on the safe side, spoke first to the director of his department, Kurt Stengel, a cultured south German who had never assumed the rigid tone of the victorious conqueror. Again, luck was on our side. When Jascha reported to the Commissariat, he did of course get "Jew" stamped diagonally across his identity card, but he was treated in a relatively friendly way. Then an inspector suddenly came out of the neighboring room, saw what was going on and bellowed: "What's this? This guy didn't register as a Jew? Lock him up!"

"I'm sorry," his colleague replied, "but the director of his German authority called and said that he guarantees, on his honour as an officer, that this man is telling the truth and that he's indispensable; in other words, he's working for the Germans."

That same evening, a colleague from Jascha's office came to our apartment. Marc Wallach was a Russian émigré, naturalized in France. After June 21 he indicated to Jascha that he sympathized with the Soviet Union. He made Jascha's work much easier. On that evening Marc Wallach told me that he had been sent by Kurt Stengel, to give me the urgent message that I should go to call upon Max Gall.

Moreover, Marc wanted Jascha to go and stay at the apartment of his girlfriend, Marie-Louise. Marie-Louise was a completely apolitical little postal employee and it appeared that Jascha would be safe staying with her, at least for the time being.

On September 20, 1941 I went to visit the Gall family in the chic 16th Arrondissement of Paris. The salon in which I was received was equipped with the typically cheerless furniture of the French bourgeoisie. Max Gall, dark-haired, round-headed, powerfully built, lively, straightforward, reminded me very much of my brother-in-law Fritz Freudenthal. A bit coarse in manner, but still likeable, he exhibited a certain intelligent charm. His wife, a truly pretty blonde native of Normandy from a French academic family, was much more reserved. I believe she found her husband's relations with us rather unsettling and she was undoubtedly somewhat anxious. But like many French women she stood by her husband in everything he did and was ready to take on any risk, if her husband thought it was important and just. These resolute women also helped save the lives of many German émigrés.

Max Gall told me first of all that my husband absolutely had to disappear. The German officer Kurt Stengel could protect him against the French authorities, but he would have to report the matter to the Gestapo. Leningrad could hold out for another two weeks at most. When the Germans had taken the city, it would be easy to prove that Jascha was a Jew and there would be no mercy for him. Then he explained to me that he belonged to a group of Bavarain Catholics, who were opposed to Hitler, above all on humanitarian grounds. It had contacts to an opposition group in Fascist Italy to which Marshal Badoglio also belonged. It called its members "gli nostra" – "our people". His group also called itself "the nostras" and most of its members were officers from Bavaria.

Gall explained the political-military situation: Leningrad and Moscow would fall before the beginning of winter and in the spring the German army would reach the borders of Persia. That would be the point at which the United States would enter the war. In the end, the Allies would prevail, because the Germans would be overextended and thus weakened. But when the United States entered the war, Hitler would no longer have to take Roosevelt and American public opinion into consideration. The barbaric racial persecution would be taken to extremes. Detailed plans for the extermination of the Jews were already complete. They would then be put into practice. He estimated my own risk, as a woman with a child, at practically nothing. In Europe one did not kill woman with small children! But Jewish men would be destroyed without exception. He offered Jascha thirty thousand Swiss francs to cross the Swiss border to survive the war there.

Of course we discussed the problem with Paul Grasse, who was in the leadership of the Party group in Paris, even though Jascha had another liaison man. Some days later I brought the answer to Max Gall: "My husband can't take your offer; he wants to keep on working for his anti-Fascists group. But we would be grateful if you could help us to support German émigrés who are especially at risk."

Now we arranged a meeting between Max Gall and the "old man", which actually led to contacts between the Bavarian group and the later Free Germany Committee.

During the next two years the "nostras" not only helped our German anti-Fascists group; we received important tips on forthcoming police actions and arrests and also about the effect of our actions on some German army officers. In January 1942 Jascha even had a conversation with a Colonel Schroeder, the commander of a hospital guard unit at a prison camp for Soviet soldiers in Bavaria. Filled with indignation, he spoke of the inhuman treatment of the prisoners. For example, they were given sawdust soup to eat, so that in three months more than sixty per cent of them had died of starvation. He was impressed by the fact that the morale of the Soviet prisoners remained unbroken from the simple soldiers to the high-ranking officers. For example, contrary to all the propaganda, there were no sexually transmitted diseases among the Russians.

In September 1941 Jascha began to lead a truly illegal existence. He had to get another identity card, because as early as autumn 1941 the authorities had regularly begun to stop young men on the street, to check their papers. I sold a valuable diamond brooch that had belonged to my grandmother and he used the money to obtain an identity card in the name of Jean Oberlin, born in Colmar in Alsace. The card looked a bit odd, but it bore a police stamp and seemed unobjectionable, after Jascha had passed a first police check. With this paper he applied for work at a translation bureau, registered with the tax office and moved into an apartment in a new building with heat and hot water, neither of which worked during the war. Jascha felt himself completely safe with this identity card until the day, a year later, when comrade Etienne, who was responsible for our illegal work, checked his papers. He turned pale and asked Jascha, whether he had really shown this card when he was looking for work and an apartment.

"Sure, why not?" was Jascha's naive answer.

Etienne began to laugh. "How much did you pay for it? These identity cards were being issued by some of the mayor's offices for a short while, but then the identification procedure was centralized and they were declared invalid. And this stamp is the best part: look at it under a magnifying glass – it's a police stamp all right – but from the office of bicycle permits. You really have more luck than sense."

However, that may have been, Jascha did have an identity, a well paid job in a translator's office and a safe apartment.

I, on the other hand, continued to live with our son André in our old apartment under my real name. I stayed in contact with the Bavarians and was part of our German-speaking group. My main activity consisted in distributing leaflets in front of German restaurants and German barracks. The difficulty in this work were the many kilometers that we had to hike through the streets of Paris. The Paris Metro had automatic doors on its cars and at its entrances and exits. This made it easy for the police to close off individual trains and stations and to set up traps, which they frequently did. We had a strict rule against using the Metro when we were carrying printed material. For female couriers, this created special problems in obtaining shoes that would hold up on the Paris pavement. Shoes with wooden soles were very unsuited for hikes of anywhere from nine to twelve miles and there wasn't even any lotion available to rub onto one's wounded feet.

In spring 1942 I too went to work as a translator at the Vermont bureau, where Jascha worked as Mr. Jean Oberlin. Under my real name, with my real papers, a German-Lithuanian woman, whose Jewish husband had fled to Switzerland because of the arrests. My colleagues and Madame Vermont, who ran the bureau, were convinced that I was having a love affair with Mr. Oberlin.

"In my day, young women with children were not in the habit of going out with other gentlemen, in the absence of their husbands," Madame Vermont observed with a shake of her head. "Mr. Oberlin, it's high time that you find yourself a woman and get married." And in the café nearby, where we often went for a drink, the good-natured owner observed that anyone could see at first glance that we weren't married, but rather young lovers. The fact that we were in love, after eight years of marriage, was the best possible camouflage for us. Only our "old man" refused to see it. He found, when we met on Sundays in the Bois de Boulogne and I had André on my arm and we were carefree, hugging and kissing each other, that we were attracting too much attention. We just laughed at him.

Meanwhile, the French Resistance had organized itself. The émigré groups were gathered into a special organization, the "Mouvement Ouvrier International", or MOI. At its head was a committee of three members, an Italian, a Pole and a Yugoslav. The German anti-Fascists also belonged to this organization and were first known as "German labor". Later their group was called the "Free Germany Committee for the West." In the summer of 1942 the German group assigned Jascha to the technical branch of the MOI where he immediately went to work as a photographer in the document section.

Soon thereafter I became a courier for the technical branch, because it was considered too dangerous for us to be working in two different groups.

An exception was made by permitting me to continue contact with the "old man", since Max Gall refused to get to know a new liaison person. I moved into Jascha's new apartment and left André in the care of French comrades who were later active in the Resistance.

My memories of the years 1942 and 1943 ought to be serious and sad, but I must admit that that isn't the case. For one thing, we were active and fully occupied and had no time to feel resigned. And also, certainly, because we were always together and could discuss everything with each other. Our French friends continued to see us and, at our request, helped endangered, illegal German Jews and comrades. It was also possible for us to help many others, even if only with money. We were earning good money in our translation bureau without having to work for the Nazis or the French Fascists.

Our political director was Etienne. He came from Transylvania, knew all of Europe, was well educated, with a sense of humor and with the charm of the Hungarian intellectual. We were certainly his favorites, because in difficult situations we tried to find solutions and were not simply negative. And so in regard to discipline he would look the other way and allowed us freedoms and possibilities which he certainly did not grant the others.

In a short time our apartment was transformed into a studio, in which every kind of photo reproduction, counterfeit stamps and even zinc plates were fabricated. For five months the draftsman stayed in our apartment. That simplified the work, but it created an additional security problem. Michel was a Pole. He was being sought for taking part in a student action. Just like Jascha he had the ability to master complex technical problems. In a short time he became like a brother to us.

He was always in a good mood, even when I once didn't manage to find cigarettes for him. When I came home in the evening, he had already cleaned up the apartment and was ready to help me in the kitchen. Fortunately he had no prejudices in the matter of food. He enjoyed the millet that I purchased at the pet store for birdseed and which we separated from the hulls ourselves, as much as he did the cat roast that I prepared in a laboratory I knew or the fish paste made of ground up bones, heads and salt, which was quite tasty served on lettuce leaves.

Michel's cleverness was nearly fatal to us. Among his paraphernalia he found a bottle of purple stamp ink that he urgently needed. It had dried up and he tried to dissolve it with water, but he used too much water and the resulting ink was too thin and runny. He wanted to thicken it again and since it was a nice warm summer day and the sun was shining, Michel set the opened ink bottle out on a window ledge, to let the water evaporate. But a gust of wind knocked the bottle over and it flew from the ninth story down onto the street. When we came home, we found a dark puddle on the street, but we didn't think about it. We got the point very quickly, however, when we encountered the outraged janitor's wife. When the bottle fell, ink poured out of it and splashed all over the washing that had been hung out on the balcony just beneath us. "You don't set an ink bottle on the window sill and then just walk off and leave it!" stormed the janitor's wife, who was unaware that we had a third party in the apartment.

Michel turned pale and began to shake and when we told him about the accident with the washing, he was, for the first time, truly depressed. Very humbly and shamefacedly we presented ourselves before the wrathful lady and offered her compensation in money, which fortunately she accepted.

While she was expressing her astonishment that the ink spots couldn't be removed with the usual cleaning fluid, we took a hasty leave. Down on the street, the ink blot could be seen for a long time, but to our amazement and Michel's relief, no policeman ever noticed a thing.

Franka, an active comrade, was also a courier for the MOI. Her husband, a former fighter in Spain, had been deported that winter. She and her nine year old son were supposed to be arrested as Jews. At the last moment both fled to our apartment. They stayed there until the child had been installed safely at a boarding school. Then we learned that Franka urgently needed an operation on her thyroid gland because of a malignant tumor. A surgeon was found who was prepared to operate on Franka in his private clinic under a fictitious name. However, he made it a condition that she had to leave the clinic after three days at the latest, because the police regularly inspected the patients. So it was necessary to shelter her for a while in a safe place, where she could be cared for and, if necessary, be given an injection. This was easier said than done. Franka was able to convince her boss and ours, Etienne, that our apartment was the only safe place. She was a slender little person, who looked undernourished under normal circumstances, but when she came tottering out of the clinic, deathly pale and supported by a nurse, I was convinced that I wouldn't be able to get her to our apartment. Motorized taxis were not available; instead I had procured the sort of "taxi" that had taken their place: a tandem bicycle driven by two riders, pulling a two-wheeled trailer behind it, onto which a big crate had been mounted. The crate contained two seats. We had to lift Franka into the crate. The seats had no back rests and during the entire trip I had to hold her up.

The two bicyclists also had the feeling that their customer might tip over at any moment. When I went into labor in 1941 and was taken to the hospital, there were already no automobiles available and we had to use exactly the same type of crate. It was thirty degrees centigrade in the shade then and the two cyclists were pedaling at an exceptionally fast pace, so that they were bathed in sweat by the time we got to the maternity hospital. They must have been afraid that I was going to give birth in their crate. This time the men rode very slowly and kept turning around to look and breathed a sigh of relief when we reached our destination. They helped me to carry the almost unconscious Franka into the apartment.

During the following days and nights we felt very insecure. Twice our patient had a heart attack during the night and Jascha had to give her an injection. We were frightened during those nights and feared for the life of the patient, of course. But another thought was almost more terrifying, what would happen if Franka died and we had to bury a body without a fixed address and with fake documents? Fortunately Franka was tougher than she looked and after ten days she was up and walking and even helping me with the chores. One day the municipal water inspector appeared and Franka was so incautious as to open the door. He wanted to see what was wrong with our bathroom.

Although there was no hot water and the apartment was not heated, we had used, during the six months of winter, as much water as a municipal public bath. "In this cold weather you can't have been bathing three and four times a day," he barked at poor Franka. Besides, he told her, some of the other tenants had also complained that we kept the water running every night.

There was a good reason for that. We could only develop our films, photographs and zinc plates at night when we were at home and that required a lot of water.

Franka, fortunately, caught on at once and, good psychologist that she was, reacted with the requisite speed. "Oh," she said, "just look at me, I've been sick for months and my bed clothes have to be washed every day. And something's wrong with the pipes in this building. Come and take a look at the toilet, the tank is leaking and it never stops flushing."

The inspector shook his head skeptically, but confronted with the spectacle of Franka's obviously pitiful condition, he left without writing a protocol.

When we came home that evening, we found Franka trembling from a new heart attack. We decided that our apartment was not an appropriate residence for an extremely courageous person who, however, needed care that we could not provide.

In June 1943 our Russian friend, Dick Pakrowski, asked to come and talk to us. It was his second trip from Germany to Paris, but this time he was determined not to return to his factory job in Berlin. In Berlin, Dick had been in constant contact with an engineer who was working for the English intelligence service. Dick had provided him with important data. Before Dick left Berlin, the engineer had come to him and asked him to do everything possible to put him in touch with the Gaullists and, through them, with the British. Following an arrest, he had, some time before, lost his contact with London. In the meantime, he had learned about a lethal secret weapon that was scheduled to be used against England within the next few months. It was being developed in the high frequency department of the Siemens electrical plant in Berlin.

Dick had no connections to the Gaullists, so he asked us to try and do what was necessary.

We discussed the matter with the "old man" and with our boss Etienne. But, due to arrests within recent weeks, the MOI contacts to the Gaullists and to London had been disrupted.

"If you can manage to avoid involving us, then you have permission to make French contacts, provided they're safe." was the answer from both of our mentors.

But who, among the French people known to us, was a Gaullist, or had connections to London? My first attempt, to reach the appropriate circles through my old professor of viticulture, a conservative Catholic, ended in failure. He recommended a gentleman whom he believed to be a genuine French patriot with the requisite contacts. Somehow I didn't trust this recommendation. I decided not to call upon the gentleman. Fortunately, because it later turned out that he was working both for Petain and for the Germans. Most of the French people with whom we were in contact were politically too far to the left to work with the Gaullists, or were themselves already in jeopardy.

And then came the illumination. We remembered our personal friends Adrien and Simone Chaye. They were upright, patriotic French people from good, middle-class Breton Catholic families, with even a real bishop among their relations. They were also open-minded and convinced that Fascism was ruining Europe and France. We had gotten to know the Chayes in 1937, when we were hitchhiking along the Loire valley, visiting the chateaux. They took us on a three-day trip, as their passengers, after which we were invited to stay at their home. Zin, as his friends called him, was a competent engineer, specializing in high frequency and optical equipment. In the years before the war, his company had sent him to America, the Soviet Union and Germany and his wife had traveled with him whenever possible.

He was brilliant in his field, but in all practical and psychological matters he left the decisions to Simone, which resulted in a harmonious marriage. Simone was a tall, golden blonde Breton, whose charm was equaled by her originality. While her husband presented a modest, plain appearance, she made an impression of elegance, in part because she always followed the latest French fashions. We always laughed till we cried whenever she told about her trip to Bitterfeld in 1938 with her husband, who was supervising the assembly of various devices for the Agfa company. In this small, central German provincial town, the children ran after her in the street, chanting "French woman! French woman!" In the modest hotel where they stayed and where they ate, the men seated at the other tables in the dining room stared at her incessantly, until she told them, "Monsieur, n'oubliez pas votre soupe, elle sera encore plus mauvaise, si elle devient froide." "Don't forget your soup, Monsieur, it will be even worse when it's cold." She provoked the Philistines of Bitterfeld by using every French cosmetic she could find, including blood-red nail polish. Even though we seldom saw eye to eye politically, in regard to Hitler's Germany we and the Chayes were in full agreement. At the beginning of the war we had lost sight of Zin and Simone; he was working in England. When we met them again and established, after some cautious conversation, that their political ideas were not so very different from ours, we were pleased. Given everything we knew about them, we could assume that Zin had contacts among the Gaullists and to England. We were of course taking a risk but our feelings and convictions proved right.

Zin took what we told him very seriously. He had his own theory about the Nazis' so-called secret weapon and although it later turned out to be wrong, it still led him onto the right track.

A representative of Siemens was a client of our translation bureau. I received instructions to question him unobtrusively about certain of his firm's products – a relatively simple assignment. A month later, Siemens' Wernerwerk plant in Berlin-Tegel was bombed. But, as Zin told us a short time later, the action came too late – the secret weapons had been moved two weeks before to an unknown destination.

We had dinner together with the Chayes and they introduced us to their friends, the engineer René Labord and his wife. After we had eaten, Simone and Mrs. Laborde withdrew and we were left alone with the gentlemen. Laborde came straight to the point: he asked us where Peenemuende was and what was there. We trotted out all our store of information about the German Baltic seacoast and described Peenemuende as a tiny fishing village where, as the saying has it, the foxes wish each other a good night. Laborde persisted in his questioning: "Is there any industry there? Any significant harbor installations? We've received orders for Peenemuende that look like they're intended for the aircraft industry."

Jascha and I were in agreement that in the summer of 1937 the area had been populated by vacationers from Berlin, but that there was no sort of industrial infrastructure. Orders of that kind had to have a military purpose. Zin and Laborde were satisfied with our information.

A few weeks later, at the end of August 1943, we were informed that the military base at Peenemuende had been destroyed. His Majesty's Government thanked us for the information that we had provided, which had helped to identify the location of the secret weapon.

That was all. Despite an explicit testimonial from René Laborde, we have never been officially recognized by the French government as Resistants.

In September 1941 Max Gall had predicted that all Jewish men were going to be exterminated. At that time, the Bavarian officers already knew about these plans. However, they were convinced that in Europe no one would dare do the same thing to women with small children. But a year later, in autumn 1942, the authorities began systematically arresting foreign Jews, the elderly, invalids and also women with small children. All those arrested were taken first to a transit camp at Drancy, the same Parisian suburb where we were hiding our son André. After a few days or weeks these people were loaded onto cattle cars and transported to the east under inhuman conditions. The arrests were carried out by the normal French police. They took people from their homes in the early mornings, loaded them onto trucks and turned them over to the Germans at Drancy. In two or three Parisian arrondissements, the inspectors belonged to the Resistance. On the eve of a planned mass arrest, they sent their officers to tell people that they should get ready to be taken away the next morning. As a result of these warnings, families were found sitting with their children on their packed suitcases, waiting for the transport. Even after the first leaflets had been distributed about the camps in Poland, many Jews still believed that they were merely going to be resettled in ghettos.

The Bavarian Catholic officers' group informed us twice that transports were imminent. We tried to persuade two young Romanian women and several seventeen and eighteen year old children of Polish women comrades to go undercover. We promised to get papers for them – all to no effect. Comprehension only began, when adults and children were herded into the cattle cars with curses and blows in the most brutal way.

During the first transports the ventilation hatches in the cattle cars had not yet been covered with barbed wire. Several mothers succeeded in shoving their children out through these hatches. Every French railroad man who got hold of one of these children took it in his arms without hesitation and carried it to safety. At no time, not even in 1942, when the Resistance was still barely organized, did the sheltering of Jewish children represent a major problem. Among country families, in the cities, in boarding schools, in cloisters; they were sheltered everywhere and people were at pains to obtain ration cards and took clothing for them.

Lilli with André.

We had already placed our son André with his correct papers with the Delamare family in Drancy. He was a pretty, friendly child. The family adored him and the neighbors were receptive to André's special charm. The Delamares' next door neighbor was a police employee, working for the "Affaires juives", the bureau in charge of all the actions against the Jews. One Sunday, when we had both gone to visit our son and had taken him out for a short stroll, this officer came to see the Delamares and told them: "I don't have any objection to your hiding the nice little guy here, but if you don't want it to come out that he's a Jew, then for God's sake don't let the father come to see him. You can spot him for a Russian Jew from two miles off!"

There were also of course, some cases in which notorious Fascists or especially malicious neighbors, who bore some sort of grudge, would draw the attention of the authorities to an illegal Jewish child, but those were really exceptions. Although we were known in our former neighborhood and in the Latin Quarter, the university district, as émigrés and Jews, it never occurred to us to avoid that area.

We also never thought of avoiding any of our acquaintances or colleagues. I only became seriously frightened once, in 1942. While out for a walk with André I ran into the blonde technical assistant of my relative Kurt Freudenthal. The last time I saw her, in 1940, she had been with a handsome, dark-haired lieutenant of the French air force; now she was promenading with a blond giant in a German officer's uniform. She greeted me in a friendly way, but she must have seen the stricken look on my face, because she quickly took her leave of her companion and went directly to me. She was sincerely interested in learning that I had remained in Paris and was not in the unoccupied zone, like everyone else. She took an interest in André, who smiled at her enthusiastically and she admired his nice friendly appearance. Was my niece Marga safe, she asked. When I answered affirmatively, her pleasure at the news was definitely not simulated. I asked her about my brother-in-law Kurt, since we had completely lost track of him since 1940. From her, I learned that Kurt, thanks to the English woman who had also helped him in the internment camp, had apparently been evacuated from Dunkirk with the English troops. In any case he had gotten a message to that effect to his former assistant. The blonde young lady was still working; I did not want to ask where. She was silent about that and she also, fortunately, did not pose any indiscreet questions of her own.

André was not just a good-looking child; he was happy and bursting with strength. We were all the more worried when, although he was one year old, he only stood up when he had something to hold on to and instead of walking, crawled on all fours, at top speed and shouting for joy. We consulted a pediatrician. "The child is just too fat and lazy," he said. "A child that happy can't be sick." Another doctor whom we consulted, said that the problem was caused by an excessively tight foreskin, that made walking painful. If we would just get him circumcised everything would be fine. So we had the operation done in a private clinic. He spent three days in bed, until the wound was somewhat healed, but he still couldn't walk. An old lady of our acquaintance insisted that this was punishment for not having had him circumcised by a rabbi. "Is that all God has to worry about, in times like these?" we answered. In the spring of 1943 we finally had the idea of consulting Dr. Lecoeur, the orthopedist at a large children's' hospital. As soon as he saw the boy he said, "That's Pott's disease, tuberculosis of the spinal column." The only possible treatment was to maintain the spinal column in a state of complete inactivity. My poor, lively André would have to spend at least a year in a body cast, unable to move. Normally, patients with tuberculosis of the bone were sent to sanatoriums in the mountains or at the seaside, where the treatment consisted in open air or sun cures. In these sanatoriums, the children lay together on the terrace and forgot their health problems in play. Dr. Lecoeur advised against sending the boy to a sanatorium.

Food rationing, in 1943, had reached a point at which hospital nutrition was not much different from prison nutrition. Our boy would not become well on this official invalid's diet, he would starve. It would be a different matter if he could be sent to Switzerland with a Red Cross children's transport, but with our papers that was impossible. Dr. Lecoeur advised us to have André treated by a private nurse. We were able to arrange that easily and quickly.

Up till then, we had felt that we were in a privileged situation. We were together, the child was in a safe place, we had interesting jobs, were earning good money and were accomplishing useful things in our illegal activity. For the first time we began to worry about the future and we asked ourselves what would become of André if something happened to us.

More than anyone, the Galls understood our problem. Where our child was concerned, Mrs. Gall was warmly sympathetic. Max Gall promised to try to use his connections to smuggle the boy into Switzerland as part of a Red Cross children's transport. There he could be admitted to a Swiss sanatorium and treated by Swiss doctors. This was accomplished in October 1943.

It was not only André's illness that concerned us. We were afraid of the continuously expanding deportations. Mostly we would get a final postcard from Drancy, saying that the writer was leaving on a transport – and then nothing more. Thousands in every train and no one ever succeeded in sending a sign of life! To be sure, we had printed many leaflets and circulated the contents of a talk by Thomas Mann on Radio London, but the monstrosity of the Holocaust was still by no means clear to us.

We were concerned about the many arrests in our group and several times we had gone on high alert. Questions were raised about the continued security of our apartment, but our boss Etienne declared, laughing, "Teddy and Jascha's place is our last bastion – we're not giving it up quite so easily!" He reminded us constantly of the need for caution. On the other hand, we were able to obtain important documents through our French connections and our contacts to the Bavarian officers had proven useful not only to the German anti-Fascists, but also to the MOI Central Committee.

Paul Grasse, the "old man" had become our problem child. One June evening he was waiting for me in front of my translation bureau. His desperate situation explained this lack of discipline. Coming back from a meeting he saw that the French police had searched his apartment and found documents proving that he was working for the anti-Fascists and the German Communists. He had to leave the apartment at once and find a place to stay. He was supposed to meet the German comrades again in three days. I was the only one whom he could reach. He had a place to sleep for one night, but after that he needed our help. The "old man" was in luck. Marc Wallach, who had supported Jascha when he went underground, had himself, in the meantime, become suspect. Kurt Stengel, the engineer, had warned him that the Gestapo was investigating his Aryan credentials, which made Marc decide to disappear. He left his apartment, obtained a new set of papers and got in contact with the Resistance. He had left us the key and permission to use his empty apartment. We installed the "old man" there temporarily. A few weeks later we were able to organize another apartment for him, because the name Wallach might attract the police. Otherwise we only met up with him every three or four weeks, in order to keep up our contact with Max Gall.

CHAPTER IX

1943 – 1944

Arrest in France

"Why are you angry at me? I can't help it that I beat you. I had to do it. Orders are orders."

On November 21 1943 we showed up at the translation bureau at nine o'clock as always. I was sitting with the owner, Madame Vermont, in the outer office, receiving customers and messengers. Jascha, who did the larger technical translations, was in the back office where he could work undisturbed. On this particular day, however, he had an important and lengthy piece of work to prepare for the MOI. It had been agreed that the job absolutely had to be finished that very day, because the next morning Etienne wanted to come to our apartment with a leading comrade from the Central Committee of the MOI, to discuss the technical possibilities of this new procedure which Jascha was preparing. It was an exceptional situation, arising from the urgency of the problem.

At noon, Jascha announced that he had an important job to complete that afternoon and wouldn't be able to finish the technical translation he had been assigned to do until the following afternoon. A big scene with Madame Vermont followed, this translation, she said, had been ordered by an old and very good customer, whom she could not disappoint and the work in the Bureau had to come before any other obligations, including work for the Resistance. Did he really believe that his underground work was going to force the Germans to leave France one single day sooner? At this, Jascha sat down and hammered out the translation at top speed. At twenty minutes after two he slammed the finished translation down in front of the lobster red Madame Vermont and walked out with the words "There's the shit for your crappy customer!" Ten minutes later three men entered the room: one could see by the very tips of their noses that they were from the French police.

They were short, flabby-faced, sloppily dressed, two with berets, one with a fedora, which they didn't bother to take off when they came in. Without a word to Madame Vermont, two of them stood next to me, while the third opened the door to the back office and remarked: "Nobody there!" A stone fell from my heart and I answered their questions in a relatively courteous way. They wanted my handbag. I handed over my portfolio, which contained some food items and the handbag. There was a good reason for that: Etienne had told me a few days before that I had to get rid of this handbag with its false bottom, which I used for my courier work. If the police found it they would know immediately that I was working for the MOI. Two girls with that type of handbag had already been arrested.

Although I knew what that meant, instead of getting rid of the compromising article, I stuck it in my portfolio, or in a shopping bag. One of the police officers took out the handbag, inspected my identity card, the food rationing coupons, my purse and my reader's card from the Bibliotheque Nationale. "In order," he told his colleagues. Three stones fell from my heart. My identity card was genuine, but the last time it had been renewed, the renewal had been done in our studio-done so well that neither these officers nor any others ever noticed it. It contained my earlier address. The officers didn't recognize the sort of handbag it was and they didn't ask about Jascha. This made it possible for me to respond to their unfriendly questions and their snarling in a relatively calm and polite manner. Then they held a picture of Paul

Grasse under my nose and asked, very severely, "Do you know him?"

I did a lightning calculation. Above all else, I had to draw attention away from Jascha and our apartment and lead them down a false trail! "Yes," I said, "I know him, I'm good friends with him."

Where did you hide him? We know that he came to you after we found his apartment. We saw him with you in a restaurant. The groceries you've got in your handbag are certainly meant for him. He's a German Communist!"

They didn't even pay real attention to my answer, they were so convinced that I was legal and thus could afford to hide the "old man". They looked through my desk and found my address book with many foreign addresses, as well as a leaflet in German, which forecast defeat on the eastern front. Some customer or other had shown it to me and asked me what it said and I, with inexcusable carelessness, had put it in my top drawer. Play for time! I explained the story of the leaflet to them and translated the text into French. Poor Madame Vermont was rigid with horror. But all the delay accomplished nothing. After telling me a second time, that the man whom I had helped was a Communist, they informed me that I was under arrest, gathered up my things and led me away. Madame Vermont, who up to that point had treated the officers with contempt, began to weep. "But you can't arrest this young woman, she has a little child that's seriously ill and lying in a plaster cast. You can't just deprive a child of its mother!"

The police just laughed.

Because I actually was not suspected of anything, I certainly hadn't been seen with any of the comrades aside from the "old man", they didn't put handcuffs on me. My companions walked peaceably beside me. My papers were in order and I had a normal job. One officer carried my portfolio and another the oh so compromising handbag.

One thing was clear: once we got to the station, someone would discover the false bottom of the handbag and for at least six, maybe eight days I would be beaten in the hope that I would betray some meeting or other. As the inspectors were bringing me down the stairs to the Metro, I considered for a moment throwing myself under an oncoming train.

Still, there was one thing I had completely forgotten: the stinginess of French petty officials. At the entrance, the inspector gave me my handbag and said "You've got money, buy yourself a roundtrip ticket." At first, when I suddenly found the bag in my hand, I thought I had misunderstood him.

"Hurry up!" the inspector was getting irritable.

I could hardly speak for excitement. I clutched the bag tightly under my arm; I was obsessed with the idea of getting rid of it somehow. Play for time! It was already past four o'clock when we arrived at my former apartment. The concierge was new and stated at once that she didn't know me. And the woman who opened the door denied indignantly that I ever could have lived there. Now I finally consented to present my case. Yes, I was illegal, a Jew, a Soviet citizen, my husband had fled to Switzerland in 1941 and I had moved out in November 1942 when my child and I were threatened with arrest.

The first, unexpected reaction: they didn't want to believe that I was a Jew."It's quite obvious. You're a German and you've made common cause with the Communists and now you're telling us you're a Jew to throw us off the Communists."

Finally I succeeded in convincing them that no one, in 1943, was going to admit voluntarily to being a Jew, especially someone with a child. Besides, in my case this was very easy to establish, because in my German birth certificate my parents' religion was indicated.

Meanwhile we were seated in a subway car. The inspectors were loudly cursing me and everybody else who helped foreigners and Jews and Communists. The people around us were looking at me with pity, so I began talking back rather energetically, with the idea at the back of my mind, that someone would help me get rid of the dangerous handbag. When, at the Cite station, the police officers beckoned to me to get out, I quickly dropped the hand-bag on the seat and pushed my way to the exit. Two seconds later a man pressed the bag into my hand and whispered: "You forgot that." Fortunately my companions hadn't seen anything and were hurrying to the station exit. The Paris Metro stations have swinging doors that immediately close by themselves after one has passed through them. I stayed one step behind, so that the door closed behind the first two men, then I let the third one go ahead and at the moment when the door slammed shut, I dropped the handbag behind me. The officers were in a hurry; one of them said that his shift was over and he had to catch another Metro line right then. I didn't need to be admonished to run and keep up with my companions: the only thing I needed was to get as far away from that handbag as I could.

They first brought me to a big room in the Prefecture de Police, the central police headquarters, located in the center of Paris, right on the banks of the Seine. Police officers in plainclothes were seated at a number of tables, interrogating various people, yelling at them, threatening them maliciously. My companions remained standing at a table and while one of them carefully went over my papers and identity documents and examined my portfolio once more, the other began to search the pockets of my overcoat, without finding anything. "Where's your handbag?" one of them suddenly asked.

"I don't know, haven't you got it?" I asked innocently. He denied having the bag.

"Well, maybe your colleague has it; he took it away from me in the office," I said.

Luckily they had forgotten the Metro tickets and how they had given me back the handbag. Again they asked about the "old man" and named some names that I really didn't know. An unexpected question was asked: "Who was the blond young man with glasses, that we've seen with you in a restaurant so many times and that you enjoy talking to so much? "

A blond young man – so they didn't know anything about Jascha yet – not that he worked in the same office with me, or that he was my husband. "Oh," I said disdainfully, "that's a Jewish clothes dealer; he makes his living on the black market; he got my ration coupons for me. All I know is that he calls himself David."

"It looked like you were pretty good friends; we're going to take a closer look at him," they said at the end of the session.

So I had time until tomorrow. Then the important meeting in our apartment would be over. I had to hold out until then. Afterwards I would consider what to do next. One thing, above all, had become clear during the interrogation: the fact that I openly admitted to being friends with a Communist and to having helped him knowingly, had served to divert the inspectors from my activities. A political arrestee never admitted to knowing a Communist.

I was taken to one of the halls that in 1943 had been converted into cells for newly arrested prisoners.

Here at police headquarters, people were interrogated and severely beaten by the Brigade speciale, which specialized in the suppression of *"franc-tireurs"* and partisans as well as the MOI. In a room of this kind fifteen to twenty men and women were guarded by perhaps five ordinary police officers in the blue uniforms of the regular Paris police force.

Benches were the only furniture and at night you had to lie on the floor if you didn't want to risk falling off one of the narrow benches. We were taken to the toilet in handcuffs, accompanied by two policemen. Some of the arrestees had used the opportunity to escape or throw themselves out of the window.

Someone with a strong slavic accent asked about the reason for my arrest. I said that I was friends with a German Communist and the police had looked for him at my home and found out that that I was myself illegal and a Jew. I added a couple of unfriendly words about the swine of the Brigade speciale; the policeman standing next to me nodded in agreement.

Two of the French people, typical petit bourgeois types, were listening. A slender little blonde of about forty, began to moan: "We're good French citizens and keep a shop. Just because they couldn't find our sub-renter – he's supposed to be a German Communist – the cops dragged us in here." Then the husband, a wrinkled little man, started in: "You've got a relationship going with that 'Fritz'! My God, I'm a cuckold!" Throughout the evening he didn't stop whining, sobbed incessantly and wiped his eyes.

A tall blonde woman with glasses and a very severe face who looked like a German schoolteacher, was sitting in the corner.

I sat down next to her, whereupon she whispered to me that one did not admit that someone was a Communist and a German as well. I told her that the police had known that for a long time anyway and that the main thing was to divert the attention of the police, so that they wouldn't find him, because he didn't understand a word of French.

"Oh," she said, " you've been hiding our Paul."

That was the beginning of my acquaintanceship with Else Fugger, a leading German comrade who had been living in Paris under a cover name and had been arrested under that name. She became acquainted with three men who had been so badly beaten during interrogation that they were seen to be bleeding from their heads, necks and arms. The men in the room were kept handcuffed all the time. Everyone knew that they belonged to a partisan group that had killed the Nazi big shot Ritter. Ritter had been responsible for the forced transportation of French workers to Germany. Although they had been sentenced to death, the three were calm and even witty. They spoke words of encouragement to the rest of us. Somehow the police failed to notice when we improvised bandages for them and gave them food. After two days we even arranged parlor games to help us through the paralyzing waiting spells. I remember how hard we laughed during the question game "Concrete and Abstract" and "Silent Post Office". The variations in our knowledge of the nuances of French added to the complication of the games. The leader of the group, Boczow, was a Hungarian from Transylvania. On the posters that were posted all over Paris, denouncing the activities of these partisans, it could be read that he was blamed for about twenty assassinations on the railroads. From the very first moment we were like old friends. From the very first he called me "Ma jolie" – "my pretty one." Our relationship was almost a flirtation. Once he laid his head on my shoulder and said, he had never dreamed that one more time in his life he would be treated so affectionately by such a nice girl. Another time he suddenly whispered to me: "You know Etienne. You've worked for us."

Full of trust, I nodded my head.

"Did they follow you, did they find out where you work?"

I explained my situation and he smiled. "Etienne told me about you two. You've always been a ray of hope for him."

"Stay brave, I believe in you, you're bound to come through," he told me, as we parted with an embrace and a kiss. I felt, there goes my brother.

That evening a young man, a Communist as they told us, was brought in. During the interrogation the inspectors of the "Brigade Speciale" had broken several of his ribs. The guards asked us what to do with him. Else Fugger, a young man who wasn't handcuffed and I pushed two benches together and collected a couple of jackets and overcoats in order make up a bed for him. During the three days that Alfred Spitzer was at police headquarters, he was brought back every time from interrogation in such bad shape that we never took away his bed. It was kept ready for him. At night I lay down on the floor to sleep without my overcoat. Every evening one of the guards came, a different one every time, looked at me and shook his head and covered me with his own blue policeman's cape.

I will never forget a scene that was played out in that hall. A young French comrade, Cauchy, was one of the group that was arrested for the assassination of Ritter. He was kept under especially close guard, until two inspectors from the "Brigade Speciale" came to take him away to be shot, as they openly stated. Cauchy was very calm as they led him away. As he passed the benches on which Alfred Spitzer lay half conscious, he wrenched himself free, raised a clenched fist and shouted: "Long live international solidarity! Long live Communist Germany! Long live Ernst Thaelmann!"

"Allons, enfants de la Patrie." one of the men began and we all chimed in, singing along "sotto voce". Two or three of the police stood at attention, out of habit.

We quickly made contact with one another inside the hall. Between the halls there was also a buzz of information back and forth; some of it was even carried by the guards, especially the older policemen. That was how I found out the morning after my arrest that Paul Grasse had been brought in. They were blaming him for having gone to me for help and telling him that he had caused me to be arrested. Another prisoner who was being interrogated in the same room overheard the inspectors cynically asking him if he weren't ashamed of himself. An old guy like him, taking money from a young woman and starting an affair with her! Paul, in his honesty and rectitude, was terribly shocked by this and declared loudly that it was slander. I was happily married, he said and would never betray my husband.

This was a hard blow for me. Paul Grasse couldn't have known, that the "Brigade Speciale" didn't know Jascha and that I had said my husband was in Switzerland. Still, I was optimistic. The morning was almost over, the meeting in our apartment would be concluded and in the meantime Jascha must have heard about my arrest. Time had been on my side.

Towards noon I was taken to another interrogation. Two inspectors began cursing me and asking again about my handbag. When I said that one of their colleagues must have it, they became enraged. One of them had just yanked me off the chair by my hair and the other was squeezing my arm painfully, when a well-dressed gentleman came into the room and ordered, "Schlesinger, married name Segal, to me." The inspectors let go of me and this new detective, a superintendent, showed me into his office and politely asked me to sit down. Then he began his interrogation: biography, studies, occupations before and during the war; I was complimented on my French. Then he leafed through my little address book, took a long look at the many English and American addresses and asked about my family. A couple of French addresses of people to whom I had given German lessons, names of well-known and respected persons, made a visible impression on him. Probably he thought I was a Gaullist, when he said, hypocritically," Why the devil did you have to get mixed up with a Communist? Now I can't let you go; on account of this business I have to turn you over to the Germans."

"I am a Jew and a Soviet citizen and naturally I am going to help everyone who is against the Nazis. I would have helped any Englishman."

"And what about your handbag?"

I don't know where I got the gall to tell him that I had either left it lying somewhere, in my excitement, or that one of the inspectors had lost it. In any case I didn't understand why people were so interested in this handbag; when I was arrested the inspectors checked it thoroughly and removed my papers and address book.

The inspectors were called in and had to admit that they had inspected the bag thoroughly.

"Why don't you give your address. We can't hand the file on to the Germans without it."

I had nothing to lose. Jascha's presence in Paris was going to come out in the interrogation of Paul Grasse. I at least had to try to win some sympathy from the superintendent. I lowered my eyes and speaking shyly and hesitantly I told him that I wanted to tell him the whole truth, because I trusted him. My husband was not in Switzerland, but was living illegally together with me in the same apartment; he was the blond young man with whom I had been seen in the restaurant. He had to understand that I couldn't inform on my husband. He answered that he did not understand. "You were arrested yesterday afternoon. Your husband has had enough time to disappear."

"You don't know my husband," was my loyal answer. "he's a scientist, he lives in an ivory tower, he doesn't know anything about the real world, he depends completely on me for anything practical. He's sitting at home right now and crying because I'm not there."

Wonder of wonders! The superintendant looked at me pityingly, opened the door and called a guard to lead me back. Before he turned me over to the officer, he took the little address book and tossed it in the waste basket. "The Germans don't need to see that," he said quietly.

The most important thing now, I thought, was to tell the "old man" what was going on, so that our statements wouldn't contradict each other and put the "Brigade Speciale" on the right track. But to organize a brief talk with Paul Grasse I would need the help of the guards.

I consulted my Hungarian comrade, who advised me to try to set up a meeting with the "old man". Later, Else Fugger and some of the Austrian comrades reproached me for not being cautious enough. How easy it would have been for something to go wrong. I was accused of being reckless.

To be sure I was risking a sound beating or some other punishment, but I gained the possibility of avoiding something still worse. My confidence was based on my knowledge of the situation in France in November 1943. People hated the occupiers, the Petain government and all collaborators. They were beginning to hope for the victory of the English, which since Stalingrad was bound up with the victory of the Soviet Union. With few exceptions, at this point the normal police forces were on the side of the Soviet Union and the Allies and were afraid of the Germans.

I found a couple of guards who looked sympathetic and explained to them that I absolutely had to speak with the older German prisoner in the room opposite, it was a matter of life and death. And in fact, late that evening they led me down the hall to the toilet, in handcuffs as the regulations required and in the long empty corridor we met their two colleagues from the room opposite, leading Paul Grasse between them. We communicated in a few brief sentences. I explained to him that the police knew nothing about me, above all they didn't know that Jascha was working with me in the same office and that he had something to do with politics. Paul Grasse confessed, meekly, that the police believed he was having an affair with me.

"Now pay attention," I whispered, "as long as they believe that, everything's fine. For all I care, they can believe I'm turning tricks for you. If they think that, they're not interested in my political activity. Don't you worry about my reputation; if we get out of here alive, my Jascha will have no complaints." As funny as it may seem, this really seemed to calm him down.

The next afternoon, the inspectors interrogated me once again about Paul Grasse; where I knew him from, why I was helping him. Because we both gave the same account of our acquaintanceship and our first contacts, they believed me when I said I had no other political connections. Then came the questions about my apartment and my husband. When I persisted in refusing to answer, one of the inspectors suddenly said: "All right, you don't want to talk. Well, we've got a way to make you talk. Your child is in a body cast and has to be registered at some treatment center. We can check all the hospitals and find the child and take it to Drancy for deportation."

My face covered in tears, I returned to the hall. "Did you get a bad beating?" one of the policemen standing guard asked me. "No, not at all, but they thought up something far, far worse." I told him about André and the threat to look for him in the hospitals. He looked so sympathetic and so honesty shocked, that I immediately responded to his query, whether he could do something to help. "Please, go to the Institut d'Orientation Professionelle; a Madame Pieron is working there. Tell her the story and tell her that André's papers absolutely have to be altered. She's bound to know what has to be done."

As I later found out, the next day this police officer did indeed go to her. Madame Pieron, the wife of Jascha's professor, had informed a colleague, whom she believed to be in contact with Jascha. Jascha got the warning a short time later. He went to see the orthopedist Dr. Lecoeur, who was at once prepared to alter or destroy all papers relating to André.

After four days, those among us who were considered less suspect were taken to a "depot". There the prisoners were held until it was decided, whether to send them to a regular prison, to hand them over to the Germans, or to release them. The "depot" was in the cellars of the Conciergerie, underneath the beautiful old Palais de Justice. That gloomy underground vault could truly be called a "dungeon". Here those who were condemned to death in the French Revolution had begun their trip to the guillotine. Here the Queen, Marie Antoinette and the great ladies of the high nobility had been imprisoned. Now female thieves who had been caught in the act and especially the street prostitutes, who were always in trouble with the police, were lodged in these rooms. In 1790 the prisoners had been guarded by the "Garde Civile"; in the emphatically worldly Third Republic, on the other hand, the women's prison was run by nuns. Catholic sisters dressed in black received us. We were booked as politically suspect. Our group consisted of Else Fugger, two active Austrian comrades and me. There were also a blonde middleclass French woman and the French girlfriend of an Austrian comrade as well as a self-assured language teacher and a very conservative librarian from the French national library, Mademoiselle Bellet, who made the impression of having been placed on a shelf of that venerable library at the beginning of the century and forgotten there. Although her situation was not without danger, she bore all the unpleasantness with courage and humor. At no time did she distance herself from us.

Only the four of us were politically truly compromised prisoners; we all spoke passable French, were well educated, were friendly to the nuns and even went to Mass on Sunday. While the nuns sympathized with us, the real criminal prisoners were hostile towards us: they found us "too posh and too educated".

Our relationship to the prostitutes was quite different. They felt that we were just as unfairly treated as they were and most of them did not like the occupiers.

On one of the first days a young girl was brought in, apparently for the first time. She sat there, weeping bitterly. Jacquie, the spokeswoman for the ladies, rebuked her: "What are you whining about? Getting locked up? It goes with the job! Pull yourself together! Take a look at the political – they're sitting here for their ideals and not saying a word."

Jacquie, with her motherly wit, gave us many a merry hour. She was in her early twenties, a nice-looking girl with a good figure and a childlike face framed by bangs. When she was sixteen, she had been seduced by an older man and when he left her, she didn't feel able to return to her strict, middle class parents. And so she ended in a Paris brothel. For two years a German officer from Hamburg had availed himself of her services on a regular basis, a fat, cheerful man, full of pride and confidence in his army and in German victory. Now, in November 1943, he returned from home leave, asked for her, threw himself onto an armchair in her room and began to weep. Wife, child and house – they had all been killed and destroyed in one of the accursed air raids. The English were dropping incendiary bombs on the civilian population. Innocent people were being killed. That was too much for Jacquie; after all she had been in the exodus from Paris and knew what the war had done to the French civilians. Outraged, she reminded him of how a short time before he had bragged about the victories of the German army and how he had never wasted a single thought on the civilian population in all of Europe. Now all of a sudden the war had touched him personally and he was sitting there and crying like a coward!

This officer and gentleman was so shameless as to denounce Jacquie as a dangerous defeatist who was probably in the Resistance.

We had sacks of straw to sleep on and there were several water basins in the hall. In order to wash ourselves we naturally took off our dresses and shirts, for which the nuns reproved us with a censorious "Ladies, please do not show your flesh!"

Strange as it may seem, together with the prostitutes we succeeded in giving the nuns a political lesson. On an especially cold
December day, at seven in the morning, the police brought in a
group of women and children, of whom the youngest was perhaps eighteen months old. They were all wearing the yellow Jewish star and they were being taken to Drancy that evening, for
deportation. One had seldom seen such a sad picture in Paris
before. Clothed in thin, worn-out summer dresses, the children in
patched jackets either too long or too short, uncombed and dirty;
they had been dragged from their sleep, intimidated, terrified;
they sat on the benches and on the floor in the apathetic attitude
of tired and undernourished people.

At eleven o'clock as always, the nuns brought us our soup and a
piece of bread. Nothing for the women and children. We
demanded to see the Mother Superior and began a discussion
with her. Our admonitions, to practice Christian charity and at
least to take pity on the children, finally found success. With sour
faces, the nuns brought out the food. Jacquie and we politicals
monitored the action and saw to it that everyone really got something to eat.

But the dispute with the Mother Superior continued. When she
argued that the Jewish people had crucified the Savior and now had
to atone for it, we replied that Roman soldiers had crucified Jesus
and Pilate had passed sentence on him and no one today was doing
anything to the Italians on that account. And when one of us added,
that when all was said and done, the Lord Jesus himself and all the
Apostles had been Jews, the pious woman was speechless.

And then came Sunday. We went to Mass as always. The chaplain preached about the sins of the fathers, which were revenged
upon the sons, about the curse which lay upon the nation of
Israel and how an abscess had to be cut out. If even the Holy
Father did not protest the actions of the Germans, then it was not
the business of ignorant members of the congregation to pass
judgment.

The nuns left the chapel with bowed heads, but we and the girls protested loudly and resoundingly.

"Abandon hope, all ye who enter here." I said, as, four days before Christmas, we stood in the courtyard of the German military prison at Fresnes, near Paris.

"Stop that!" Else Fugger scolded me, "for a Communist there are no hopeless situations. And from now on out, be more careful. There are going to be a lot of Gaullists interned here who do not wish us well. You're still so reckless and open, you can hurt yourself and us."

This was the second time that I had clashed with Else. In the "depot" we had been taken regularly to the showers. The shower rooms were next to the catacombs of Paris. This network of branching passageways and shafts extends beneath the entire area of the city and during the fighting in 1870/71 the communards had hidden out there. While we were still in the hall at police headquarters, there was talk of the fact that several prisoners had escaped from the "depot" through the catacombs. While I was in the "depot", I still did not know, of course, what was waiting for me, but this much seemed clear: the chances of survival appeared non-existent. And so I had suggested that we two Jewish prisoners, Frederike Weizenbaum, an Austrian comrade and I should try to escape through the catacombs. Else Fugger was dead set against it. That wasn't allowed. We would get the others in trouble.

And so we remained locked in.

CHAPTER 10

1943

German military prison at Fresnes

"That was the moment of 'Radio Fresnes'."

The German military personnel, who rode with us in the prison van, turned us over to the female guards at Fresnes, the "Gretchens" as the French women called them, mostly older German women who were performing compulsory service for the duration of the war, who had been assigned to this work and carried out their task with a sense of duty but no enthusiasm.

Because French prisons were overflowing at the end of 1943, the less dangerous prisoners were lodged in the upper stories, in groups of three of four, in cells meant to hold one single prisoner. There was only one bedstead; the others had to sleep on straw sacks; during the day these were piled on top of each other and were used as a seat. When the guard unlocked the cell door, she tried to explain the rules to me in a kind of German-French jargon.

She admonished me to be "very proper, not to throw anything – sweep up, fold the blanket nicely". When I answered her in German, her mouth hung open, but then she became quite friendly. The reaction of my three new fellow prisoners was different. They were shocked. One of the women came up to me, as soon as the door had closed behind the guard. "Vera Obolenski," she introduced herself and gave me her slender hand. "Why do you speak such fluent German? How did you get here? Did you work against the Nazis?" She spoke good French with a slight Slavic accent and looked like an icon come to life: dark hair, broad cheekbones, an elongated face and almond-shaped eyes. Tall and slender, she was more than an elegant, imposing figure; she radiated the austere beauty of Russian women. Ignoring Else Fugger's warnings I explained my situation to her: born in Berlin, I was married to a Lithuanian and registered as a Soviet citizen since 1940 and I also considered myself to be a Soviet citizen. I had been arrested for aiding a German Communist.

The two other women in the cell would have moved even further away from me if they could have. Vera Obolenski, however, shook my hand and said, "I am Russian, but I regard France as my home and I defend it against the occupiers with all my strength and by every means, but I feel myself firmly bound to the Soviet people who are fighting heroically against the Germans."

With those words, our comradeship was sealed. During the two and one half months that we spent together in that prison cell, it proved itself in every situation that arose.

And then the other inmates of the cell were introduced to me: a young French student, who with her friends had taken part in a silent protest march against a seizure of hostages by the Germans. The girl had resisted arrest with such determination that she was thought to be an activist of the Resistance and handed over to the occupiers. She was in fact apolitical, but convinced that the Allies were going to win the war. For this reason she fiercely rejected the Germans' suggestion that she might work for them. They then decided to let her stew in her own juice at Fresnes for a while, in the hope of wearing her down. But what she saw at Fresnes reinforced her anti-German attitude.

The third inmate suffered from sciatica and the only bed was reserved for her. A short, slender person, modest, clothed in black, in a pullover she had knitted herself. Even in prison she was occupied with needlework that the German guards had given her.

In the eight months of my stay at the German army prison, there were always some French women who fabricated the most beautiful crochet and needlework and the most complex knitting patterns for the Gretchens. This had the great advantage that many cells contained needles and thread and also shears and other implements that had a multitude of uses. We could open the windows secretly, sew papers into our straw sacks and tap out signals. The cells were decorated with scraps of wool and other materials. For a long time our cell wall was decorated with a tricolor made of wool remnants. Also, the Gretchens liked us and we got such precious things as playing cards and matches to light our cigarettes.

Our sick lady sewed quite industriously and was cheerful. Her husband was an engineer employed by a big company and a Communist, who some time ago had formed an organization to protect the workers in his plant from being sent to Germany as forced laborers. The occupiers finally caught on that most of the requisitioned workers were disappearing because the engineers were falsifying the personnel lists.

She told us how, a week before, at five in the morning, there had been a knock on the door of their little house. Her husband had had just enough time to climb out of the window in his underwear and escape into a neighbor's garden when the French police and the Gestapo broke down the door and burst into the bedroom; in a rage, they yanked her out of bed, searched through the whole house and realized that the husband had escaped. For the previous ten days she had been suffering from a severe attack of sciatica and had been bedridden, unable to move. But now she was in such a state of shock and fear that she no longer felt her pain. She was able to stand and dress herself and walk out to the police car unaided. They told her that she would stay in prison until her husband was arrested. Now, a week later, she said that she was ready to stay there till the war ended, if her husband would just stay uncaught. Her sciatica had started up again, but she could live with that, too. We were very fond of this small, courageous woman and she trusted Vera and me. After the Christmas Mass, which the prison chaplain Paul Steinert celebrated despite all the difficulties created by the Gestapo, she poured out her heart to us. Her husband had refused to be married in church. From the Catholic point of view she was therefore not married, was living in sin, could not take communion and could not receive absolution of sin. In peacetime she had had a happy marriage and had never suffered on this account. At the beginning of the war her husband had been mobilized, then came the cease-fire and for a long time she had gone without news from him. In despair, she had gone to church one day and had gone to confession.

Among other things, she confessed that she had not married in church and she asked for absolution. The priest became angry; he unloosed a storm of abuse against unbelievers and her and all women like her who lived in sin; he threatened her, saying that there could be no divine grace for her and he finished by ordering her to leave the church. Here in prison she still suffered from being estranged from her church.

Vera and I discussed her problem. One of Chaplain Steinert's sermons had caught my attention. He had presented the very meager Christmas message of Pope Pius XII in a serious and compassionate way and had enlarged upon it, emphasizing that Christ had come especially for those who suffered innocently and who were tortured by the enemies of mankind.

We agreed that he sympathized with the prisoners and we advised our good Catholic to confide in him. A short time later he summoned her from the cell and after half an hour she came back radiant with joy. She had confessed her troubles to him and even declared that she was aware of her husband's political activities.

The chaplain had given her the absolution she sought, under the binding condition that after the war she would make up for the neglected church marriage. Three weeks later she was released and I don't believe that she ever found her husband.

I quickly adjusted to Fresnes. It was a relatively modern prison. Every cell had a flush toilet. The pushbutton that activated the flush could be unscrewed and then we had a speaking tube running from the top story to the cellar, forming a kind of telephone between the floors. In the fourth story, above us, the cells contained female military personnel who had been locked up on orders from the military authorities: women who had been drafted into the service, communications technicians – the so-called "grey mice" – who had overstayed a furlough, or who had been caught in bed with a Frenchman.

Or perhaps they had been caught selling military supplies. Once when we were using our telephone, one of them must have been sitting on the toilet. The lady let out a big yell and called the guards, to tell them that the French women were talking to each other. Fortunately the sergeant responsible for our floor was an East Prussian named Proede, a truly good-hearted, humane man with a sense of humor. I owe it to him, that I wasn't thrown into an isolation cell at least once a month. He unlocked the cell next to ours with a lot of noise and cursing and demanded loudly that the women there tell him what they were up to. Meanwhile, we got the flush button screwed back on and when he got to our cell, we were sitting nicely on our straw sacks.

There was still another communication system in our house: the heating system. The hot air ducts, about seventy centimeters in width, ran through all the floors with a ventilator in every cell that could be opened or closed. We used these ducts as a kind of tube postal service and sometimes as a telephone. From time to time we got Red Cross packages which held soap and cotton and some prisoners could even receive limited quantities of underwear and food from their families. We could borrow books from the prison library. On the other hand, there were women whom the Gestapo had ordered to be placed in solitary confinement. No mail, only the meager prison ration, no Red Cross package, no needle, no soap, no book, no warm blanket. The Protestant prison pastor had even refused to visit a Protestant Dutchwoman who was in an isolation cell.

Through the air ducts, contact was quickly made with these prisoners. We not only sent them the news and held conversations with them, we passed food items, soap and even books into their cells, tied to a string. This tube post was used throughout Fresnes. After the war, when the heating system was overhauled, a warehouse full of stuff was found inside it: dried bread, cheese, canned goods, nail care kits, a pair of pincers, even a handwritten manuscript.

The technical difficulty consisted in the fact that the ventilators of the air ducts were high up, almost right under the ceiling. Next to the ventilator a shelf was fastened and one could either lie on this shelf or hang on to it. Since I was more athletic than my cell mates, I had them give me a boost and I would climb onto the shelf.

One evening, while I was just letting something down and was hanging onto the shelf in a very uncomfortable position, the cell door was suddenly unlocked. Vera and the student turned around and let go of my legs. I fell onto a corner of the bed. Our sick French woman cried out in pain. The guard was speechless. Vera Obolensky reacted promptly: "We were trying to clean the shelf, lots of dirt, lots of dust!" she explained, smiling. That seemed to make sense to the Gretchen. Our cell was very nice and clean, she said, but we needed to be more careful!

There was a third means of communication in Fresnes. I learned about it on my very first evening. The women's building was directly across from the men's building. During the day one could see if the jalousies were open in one of the windows in the building across the way. In the twilight, on the other hand, before the spotlights came on, the windows could not be seen. Also, during the sacred dinner hour, it appeared that not all of the guard posts were manned. That was the moment of "Radio Fresnes".

It mostly started with the men calling messages out of the window. Warnings, personal communications, but also news of the victories of the Soviet army and the Allies, which were greeted with Bravo! and the usual "on les aura!" – we'll get them!

Between Christmas and New Year the news came, that Vera's husband had been arrested and was in Fresnes. Vera wanted to send him a greeting. She pulled herself up on the window ledge and yelled through the blinds, but her voice was too weak. She asked me to try for her. Holding on to the window, I used my stentorian voice, for which I had so often been rebuked at home and shouted out the news. Immediately the reaction came from across the way: "Verushka! Salut! Courage! We're going to win!"

Now I had a steady job in the cell. I passed on communications for all my immediate cellmates and called messages, that had reached us from the upper stories, to the men and repeated calls from the men that had reached only us, in our location in the middle of the building. Naturally we posted a lookout at the door, but I feel sure that I can also thank Sergeant Proede for the fact that I was never caught.

New Year's Eve 1944 is especially vivid in my memory. The guards relaxed a little. Throughout the evening, news and good wishes were broadcast over "Radio Fresnes". At midnight, a strong voice called out: "1944 – the year of our victory!"

Suddenly we heard from the men's side: "Allons enfants de la Patrie, le jour de gloire est arrivé," and immediately other voices joined in: "contre nous de la tyrannie," and now the bright voices of the women rang out, "aux armes, citoyens, formez vos batail-lons!" And we four too sang the Marseillaise with loud voices.

Vera and I held each other tight with one hand and raised the other hand in a clenched fist.

A couple of nights later we heard whistling from the building opposite. A melody. Now I could recognize it. The Warszaw-ianka. Very clearly: "Hostile storms rage through the air, threatening clouds obscure the light." Quiet. I tried to keep whistling the tune, even if it sounded weaker: "Though pain and death await us now, duty calls us forth against the foe." I stopped. And again the whistle came from over there: "We have kindled the shining flame of freedom high above our heads." Silence. When I began the next verse, Vera whistled with me: "The flag of victory, of the liberation of the nations, which leads us safely in the final fight."

The next evening the whistling came again from across the way: "Brothers, to the sun, to freedom." I chimed in: "Brothers, upward to the light." Silence. And then the end of the song came from over there. And so it went now, every evening. As soon as it got dark, my unknown comrade began to whistle. The first bars and then he would wait until I continued, often with Vera's help. Then he would either take up the melody again, or end it. "The young guard" was sung, "Red Wedding." "Avanti populo," the Russian partisan song, "We were born to perform deeds," "The night has passed and the dawn awakens, the red fleet moves full steam ahead." And then: "Madrid the beautiful," and "The sky of Spain spreads out its stars above our trenches." Now I knew, that a German who had fought in Spain was sitting over there. Now I often called out greetings to him. On some evenings I began by singing the song we had in common. And so it went for two months. Then, one evening, nothing. I waited, I began to whistle – nothing. I tried again – an anxious wait. And then suddenly a very clear French voice: "The German comrade, who whistled every evening for the German woman comrade, was taken away on a transport today. He sends her the most fraternal greetings. And I greet the comrade too. Long live international solidarity! We shall win!"

I wasn't the only one who wept that evening. My fellow prisoners had tears in their eyes, too.

One day Vera told me her story. She had helped to organize an information network that worked directly for London and de Gaulle, in cooperation with a group of conservative French nationalists. The attack on the Soviet Union and the treatment of the Soviet prisoners of war had motivated her husband and some other Russian émigrés to volunteer as interpreters in the prisoner of war camps. These men wanted to form connections with the Soviet internees and help them. Since the previous summer these prisoners had been used in the construction of defensive installations and bunkers on the Atlantic coast, so that her husband and others had the opportunity to gather precise data on the so-called Atlantic Wall. A leading member of the organization had turned informer and Vera, together with a woman who was her best friend and two of their fellow activists had been arrested. In Vera's handbag an envelope was found containing detailed plans of the Atlantic Wall. While the other arrestees were badly beaten, the SD officers (members of the "Sicherheitsdienst", or security service) treated the elegant and beautiful Vera with unusual respect. Perhaps, because she was such a grand lady, from one of the most noble families; perhaps too because she displayed such coolness and self-assurance. Yes, someone had brought her the envelope. Of course she hadn't opened it, she lied. It was meant for her friend Pyotr, with whom she had secret meetings: her husband mustn't find out about that. As they often did, the police believed the beautiful woman.

They asked where the meetings took place. She indicated the public square in front of the Russian Orthodox church in Paris, on Sunday morning after early Mass. On Monday they brought her to SD headquarters.

Three young men were shown to her, all named Pyotr, all of whom had been picked up on the previous day at the indicated place. She knew one of them and admitted it at once: he was a well-known member of the White Guard and had worked closely with the Germans since 1940. Apparently he had protested against his arrest and had been beaten up, since his face was bloody. When he saw Vera, he got in a rage and screamed that this slut did not deserve to bear the noble name of Obolenski. She was making common cause with the Gaullists and sympathized with the Reds.

Vera stayed a while longer in the military prison at Fresnes. In spring 1944 she was sent, because of the special importance of her case, to Berlin. Until the end she gave proof of both of her courage and her pride and the Germans are supposed to have called her "Princess I don't know". In the winter of 1944/45, at Ploetzensee prison in Berlin, she was beheaded.

In the middle of January I was interrogated for the first time by the SD. The two inspectors, Brausig and Duschek, were simple Viennese police officers, who had been mobilized for the security service during the war. They carried out their police work unintelligently, relying on informers and beatings. In two months they had not even found out who the "old man" was: a former member of the Prussian state legislature. They also had not discovered that my husband had worked for a German military agency and that I worked for the central committee of the MOI.

The interrogations focused on the apartment where I had installed Paul Grasse, on our financial aid to émigrés and on where my husband had obtained his false papers. The "old man" had said practically nothing, merely what we had agreed on in regard to our alleged personal relations.

Everyone whom the "old man" and I named, was someone whom we knew to have been deported or hiding in the unoccupied zone. It struck me, that every time I gave the name of a person who had been deported; no more questions were asked about him. After a while, Brausig exclaimed, "What the hell is this! You only know people who have been deported or are living illegally – that can't be true!"

"I can't help it if you've deported all the Jews, even the most harmless ones, so that the ones who are a bit smarter go underground."

He did not reply. Although our apartment, after eight weeks, was now empty, I let him beat the address out of me, in order to distract the attention of the SD from other matters.

Brausig, who flogged me with a cowhide whip, breathed a sigh of relief when I said the address; he took my hand and when I passed out for a brief spell, he acted as if he were terribly worried.

On the next day, I sat opposite him, pale and filled with hatred. Suddenly he asked, in a friendly voice: "Why are you angry at me? I can't help it, that I beat you. I had to do it. Orders are orders. Otherwise I've treated you decently."

That sounds ridiculous, but it was the worst part of the whole business. I still think that even today every Fascist country had a special police unit for the suppression of political opposition, consisting of thugs, sadists and various criminal elements. The police let these dubious elements handle the dirty work and kept their distance from them. Thus the normal Parisian police did not take part in the atrocities of the "Brigade Speciale".

But here, in the Nazi apparatus, normal police officers, with clean records, were prepared to torture defenseless people, whom they did not even believe to be guilty, once they had received orders to that effect.

Much later I came to know an Austrian Catholic, a Mr. Pacher, the owner of a stationery store in Innsbruck. He belonged to an Austrian Catholic resistance group. At the end of December 1944 he fled over the mountains to Switzerland, just ahead of the Gestapo. He had been drafted at the beginning of 1942 and assigned to the military police. His unit, which was mainly made up of Catholics, was ordered to Poland. Its primary mission was to guard groups of priests who had been arrested in every region of Poland and who were being taken to Auschwitz. In snow and in rain, without adequate clothing and shoes, several thousand priests were marched on foot to the camp. The military police only delivered half of them to Auschwitz. After two months only four hundred were still alive.

The female guards doing obligatory service and the medical personnel also carried out their orders to the letter. They numbed their consciences by repeating what had been told them: that they were dealing, without exceptions, with French terrorists who murdered and pillaged without scruple.

The cowhide therapy, to which my back had been subjected, had a comic sequel. From childhood on, my blood had been slow to coagulate. My wounds tend to bleed for a long while, a fact which has often upset dentists and laboratory assistants.

As a child I was always covered with big brown spots, because, in my wildness, I was always bumping into things and falling down. Even a somewhat exuberant embrace from Jascha sometimes caused a blue mark on my neck or arm.

When I returned to the cell, the others surrounded me, as always when someone came back from interrogation and asked: "Did it go well? Any news?"

"Not all that well," I answered. I pulled off my dress and bared my back. I don't know why the hematomas formed so quickly, but the others assured me that my back was entirely black and blue. Vera passed out at the sight and our attempts to revive her with slaps or a wet cloth were unsuccessful for quite a while. A young girl who had been in the cell with us only a few days, hammered on the door and called for help. One of the Gretchens came running, unlocked the door and saw Vera unconscious on the floor and me, white-faced and with blue, swollen shoulders, kneeling beside her. For God's sake, you've hurt yourself," she called out, "I'll get the nurse right away." Before the nurse appeared, Vera had come to herself and insisted that I lie on the bed. I was not angry about this privilege, but I insisted that Vera take some of the concoction that went by the name of tea in Fresnes. We assured ourselves that we had each given the other a terrible fright and by the time the nurse arrived we were laughing. The nurse snapped at the guard: there was no reason to bother her at mealtime because of such nonsense. Vera uncovered my back. The guard gave a muffled scream and left the cell. The nurse examined my back. Shaking her head, she said: "Why did you get such a beating? I thought you were a German?"

The medical personnel did exactly what the SD and the Gestapo told them to do, but they acted as if they knew nothing about the tortures and kept silent about them.

In contrast to the medical staff, the attitude of the Catholic priests in Fresnes, especially that of the chaplain, Paul Steinert, was characterized by courage. One day Paul Steinert appeared in our cell, nodded to me and said: "Can I speak to you alone for a moment?" That was risky in itself. As we stood in front of the door, he said quickly:"I'm supposed to give you greetings from Max Gall. Your child is safe and in a good place. You're not to worry. Have you been treated badly?"

"No, not so far, they know very little about me. But, please pass it on that they know about our apartment and the "old man's" apartment and they can't be used anymore."

The chaplain really did pass this information on. Because he had helped many French prisoners, after the Liberation he was not interned. But he volunteered to act as a chaplain to the German prisoners of war.

Vera and I were the only ones to spend long months in Fresnes. The other women were either released after a short time or deported, so that the occupants of our cell constantly changed. In March 1944 a rotund little woman with a pretty face and big black eyes was brought in. Maria spoke French with a strong Italian accent. She told us that she and her husband ran a big delicatessen on the Boulevard Monparnasse.

Her husband was a member of the Fascist organization of the Italian consulate. In January 1944, foreseeing the victory of the Allies, he had paid a lot of money to obtain a fake identity card under a new name for himself, so that after the defeat of the Axis powers he would be able to disappear for a while. She herself was completely apolitical, but she didn't like the Nazis. She had taken in the Jewish child of a neighbor woman, when its parents were deported. Up until the beginning of February things had gone well enough, but then Maria found out, that her husband was a steady customer in a nightclub in Montparnasse and was having an affair with the woman manager. At the same time, she was warned that the lady had been a Gestapo agent for a long time and was dangerous. When Maria learned that the lady was working for the Germans, it was the last straw. She went to the bar, slapped her husband's mistress and called her a whore and a "sale boche". The next morning the Gestapo came to her apartment. They had been informed both about the Jewish child and the false identity card.

Maria and her husband were arrested and the child was taken to Drancy for deportation. "It was such a sweet, well-behaved child," Maria lamented.

When Maria mentioned the name of the nightclub, Vera became extremely upset. It turned out, that this nightclub was precisely the place where her group regularly met. They had gone there once a month to dine together. Over their dinners, they discussed important organizational matters and sometimes they left messages with this manager – with a German agent – as Vera now learned by chance.

I thought to myself, silently: meetings and dinners in nightclubs, no money worries, always the possibility of going to ground in some villa or in a chateau - the Gaullists certainly had it easy; most of them came, after all, from the wealthy bourgeoisie. For us, on the other hand, even finding a room, when we had to hide one of our comrades was an almost insoluble problem.

Every month, we had to go through a complicated process to obtain food rationing coupons – not just for the men, but also for the Jewish women and children. Once the courier delivering the cards for the infants got caught; I gave up half of André's milk ration and trembled for fourteen days until I could get new milk coupons. Among our acquaintances, we were the only ones who were earning a good wage and the money that Max Gall sent the "old man" was used mainly to bring women and children to safety. I knew from Etienne that we were in contact with the Gaullists and we did carry out some operations together, but their groups, which were so lavishly supplied, helped us very little.

As time passed, the most diverse sorts of women were brought into our cell and then disappeared. Only a very few had actually done anything.

In March, shortly before Vera was sent away, a portly older woman appeared in our cell. She sat immobile on her straw sack, sobbed from time to time and during the first two days refused to eat either the "pig soup" or the black bread. With some effort, Vera and I learned the reason for her arrest. For more than twenty years she had been the cook for a count who lived in a chateau south of Paris. She had not suffered under the occupation, or from the food shortage. The count's children and grandchildren came down frequently from Paris to visit. And now, a few days ago, the Gestapo had showed up, asking about the grandchildren. The chateau was searched from the roof to the cellar.

"They rummaged through my pantry and broke all my preserve jars and gobbled up the preserves," the cook wailed in despair. In the wine cellar the police finally found what they were looking for. Behind the shelves of burgundy and cognac the grandchildren had hidden, not only a mimeograph machine, but weapons. "Nobody knew anything," our cellmate insisted, "they were such well-bred and educated gentlefolk and the grandfather is such a calm, refined man, truly noble."

The Gestapo didn't care whether anyone knew anything or not. All the inhabitants of the chateau, the grandparents, the cook, the chambermaid, the gardener and his wife and fifteen year old daughter and a laundress: they were all arrested and hauled off to the military prison at Fresnes. After a week they were released without having been interrogated.

We nearly got placed in isolation on account of the noble grand-mother. One day while she was under arrest there was an air raid. As always the guards took the German prisoners into the bombproof cellar where they waited for the "all clear" together with most of the guards. The French and the political prisoners, however, remained locked in their cells. Of course we used the opportunity. Radio Fresnes started broadcasting on every wave-length, as it were. Messages and greetings were delivered, the victories of the Allies were analyzed, we even greeted the airplanes and the bombs that were dropped by cheering and jumping for joy. We knew that the German military installations in Paris were the primary targets.

At the first sound of the siren, the noble lady in the next cell was overcome by a crying fit and screamed from fright.

The guard, who was actually quite nice, but also took her duties seriously, went to get the captain, to decide whether or not to take the old lady down to the cellar.

As the two of them passed by our cell, they could hear us cheering and jumping up and down and stamping our feet. Vera and I were dancing for joy: Vera was wearing a slip and I only had on panties and a blouse. "These two like it when the civilians get bombed," the guard said severely, shoving the officer into the cell. He was an elderly man who made a rather friendly impression. We became silent, but stood with heads proudly erect, confident of victory. No one seemed to see the comic side of the situation.

Smiling, the captain declared: "It's all the same to us, if the English kill French women and children, but you really don't have any reason to be pleased with the English air raids."

"Not so." I answered. "the English are our allies; that's why we're locked up here. Of course we're happy when they attack. Besides, so far there haven't been any civilian casualties."

He looked at me in astonishment. "What's your nationality?" I said I was a Lithuanian.

"Then all you need to do is behave rationally and you can lead a normal life, anytime you want. Why are you, a Lithuanian, getting mixed up in the French resistance? We treat you decently here. Of course, if you rebel against us and go around yelling, I have to punish you – don't you understand that?

"I am a Jew and no matter how I behave, you are going to deport me in any case. You are the captain of Fresnes and you have me locked up here and I am your prisoner and do everything I can to defend myself. Those are the rules of the game."

The Gretchen's mouth hung open. How could someone talk that way to the captain? But he said, in a friendly tone, "Then you will understand, if we punish you." He left the cell with a polite greeting and went next door to fetch the old lady .

I translated the conversation into French for the others. The cook began to cry and Vera was worried. Solitary confinement in Fresnes was pretty bad.

The air raid alarm lasted for about an hour and contrary to our usual practice we sat quietly on our straw sacks. All clear! Next door the noblewoman was locked into her cell again. The cook began to cry again.

Our door opened. Two guards were standing there. "Inspection!" one of them snapped. "Inspection?" asked the other. "Aren't we taking the one with the smart mouth to solitary?"

"No: orders from the captain, no punishment," her colleague sighed.

Before that sad morning at the end of March when Vera was ordered to get ready for the transport, Marthe Lebon was brought to our cell. She too became a real comrade to me. When they brought her in, she bore the marks of Gestapo brutality on her face and her neck. Marthe was a big, strong girl, eighteen years old, with a friendly face and friendly eyes which shone with honesty and kindness. People always imagine French women as elegant, sophisticated, quick-witted, erotic and not very domestic – this cliche hardly applied to the young girls of the prewar period. Marthe, a banker's daughter from a very well-to-do family, was simple and very innocent, a good cook and a thrifty housewife; she had managed her widowed father's household single-handed.

Father Lebon was a personal friend of General de Gaulle. Acting as de Gaulle's representative, he organized a network that was in direct radio contact with London. His older daughter and his son-in-law had already been arrested in 1943 and Marthe's sister had given birth in Fresnes. The baby, a girl, was given the name "France". Lebon was able to get his grandchild out of Fresnes and to bring her to a safe place. At the beginning of 1944, the child's parents were deported to Germany. Marthe and her younger brother kept on working. Marthe was arrested in the office where the radio equipment was kept. The Gestapo set up a trap there and the brother was taken when he brought in a suit-case full of weapons that the English had dropped the night before. My brave little Marthe: the beatings and her own fate hardly seemed to bother her, but she was terribly worried about her brother.

After the fortunes of war turned against Hitler's army, the treat-ment of prisoners began to change. Marthe told us that an agree-ment had been reached at the end of 1943, between de Gaulle's government in exile and the German army, to the effect that members of the FFI, the "Forces Francaises de l'Interieur", fight-ing inside France, would only be sentenced to death when they were found with weapons. Otherwise they would "only" be deported. Marthe's brother, however, had been carrying a whole suitcase full of weapons and the office was a weapons distribu-tion point.

Our hearts were pounding when Marthe was taken to Paris for interrogation. It was a long and anxious day. Late in the after-noon Marthe appeared, smiling and waving a big package. Things had gone well, she didn't know what was going on, but she had even seen her brother. She had been told that both of them would be deported to Germany. Marthe shared the contents of her package in comradely fashion. Relieved, we lay down to sleep.

While the others were sleeping, Marthe crept over to me and slipped a chocolate drop into my mouth. A moment later I cried out. Marthe came back to my straw sack.

"There's a little cylinder in the chocolate drop, with a message in it," I said.

When daylight came, she was able to remove the wax coating from the little roll of paper and read it. Her father wrote her, that he had a contact in the Gestapo and that everything had been done to insure that she and her brother would not be treated as armed partisans, but as normal prisoners. Marthe turned pale. "My God," she said. "I offered that guy from the Gestapo a chocolate; thank goodness he turned it down." I told her one shouldn't be too generous and we both laughed.

As we learned after the war, the Gestapo big shot was an art lover. Mr. Lebon, in order to ransom his children from the death penalty, had purchased two pictures for two million francs. The pictures had been deposited under the name of the Gestapo officer with a Parisian art dealer who acted as a middleman for the Germans. When the Germans abandoned Paris, the "art lover" had to leave the pictures behind. The art dealer, who had handled a number of similar transactions, felt that he was compromised by being in possession of the pictures. He applied to Mr. Lebon and told him that since he had paid for the pictures, they must belong to him. Mr. Lebon however was of the opinion that the pictures were, in law, the property of the Republic of France. The de Gaulle government had originally provided him with the money to bribe the Gestapo officer. And indeed, everything had gone well and his children had survived. As an honest man, he took the pictures under his arm and brought them to the Ministry of Finance.

At the Ministry he was, initially, treated like a crook. Nobody ever voluntarily gave anything to the Treasury; this had to be some kind of swindle. He was only allowed to leave after an interrogation lasting many hours and then with much shaking of heads and still under a cloud of suspicion.

Vera and I had formed a united front, but Marthe and I were bound by real camaraderie. Marthe had been brought up to believe in the Republic and in democracy. Together, we sang songs of the French Republic and Russian songs, but Marthe also knew all the French folksongs, which she sang with a pleasing voice. We began to rewrite well-known songs. To the melody of the Carmagnole we sang "Monsieur Hitler made a threat; All the Frenchmen will be dead!" And I made some new verses to the tune of "John Brown's Body":

Même à Fresnes on peut sourire
même en prison on peut rire
il y a bien de choses pires
si cela ne va pas, sourions.

Ce jour-là nous pourrons rire.
Nous aurons tous le sourire
mais pour eux ce sera bien pire
je ne crois pas qu'ils survivront.

English translation:
Even in Fresnes we can smile
Even in prison we can laugh
There are things that are much worse
If it doesn't work out, let's smile anyway
In the future we'll be able to laugh
Everyone will be able to smile
But for the others it will be worse
I don't think they will survive

The text was passed on through the window, through the water pipes, through the heating ducts and found a general response and many prisoners sang it during the air raids.

After a while we noticed that across the way in the men's wing a hand was moving behind the window pane and writing letters of the alphabet in the air. We could clearly recognize "bon jour". We took a handkerchief and began to write as well, in reverse script which was hard at first. But after a couple of days it went quite well. "How are you? Are you in isolation?"

"My name is Jean, I come from Algiers, I'm in isolation and exceptionally dangerous."

We soon had regularly scheduled chats and sent each other good night kisses and words of encouragement. We also forwarded news for third parties.

At the beginning of May a vulgar looking girl came into the cell. She spoke some broken German and used some sexual expressions that I had never heard before. She had worked in the kitchen of a big mess hall and had an affair with a German corporal. "They threw me in the slammer 'cause I gave him a dose of clap."

We very quickly became suspicious, especially when the girl, who otherwise seemed so primitive, began to ask a lot of very complicated questions.

The next day, as I stood at my observation post at the window, I noticed that Jean was writing extremely fast. At first I couldn't read what he wrote, but with repetition it became clear: Please don't answer, an informer has been infiltrated into your cell.

When I was brought back to the Avenue Foche for interrogation, Armand, a young Pole, was sitting in the inspectors' room. Armand had been my liaison man for a while.

I denied knowing him, of course. When they pointed out to me once again that I definitely had to know him, I shook my head. "Come on now," Inspector Dushek said menacingly, at which Armand stated: "I know this woman well. She's a German émigré. She joined the group in autumn 1941. For about a year she led a group that distributed leaflets in German at barracks and restaurants where German troops go."

The only thing I could do was to confirm the accuracy of the information. Brausig, the other of my two interrogators, accused me of lying to the police and asked if I weren't ashamed. "No, I'm not," I answered.

The two inspectors went out to eat. They left me sitting in the outer office and said, threateningly: "When we come back, if you're still this stubborn, we're not going to fool around. We'll do this the short way." The threat made me fear for my life and it may have impaired my ability to think clearly. After a while Armand was brought back to the room in handcuffs. He sat behind me; a high backrest was between us. Still, I could understand him when he whispered: "I'm sorry I dropped you in it. But I really didn't know that they hadn't arrested you in connection with the German group and that they didn't know anything about you." "It's not so bad," I consoled him. As long as they don't know anything else, I thought.

But then came the second blow. "Etienne was arrested last week and they were looking for him. Now they're looking for his liaison people."

I should have been warned, if only because we were able to whisper here; nevertheless I made an unpardonable mistake. I said to him: "Can you give Etienne a message?"

At first he resisted; then he said he would try.

"The photographer's wife does not know Etienne."

The inspectors returned from their meal and the interrogation resumed. Brausig wrote and Dushek paced back and forth. Unimportant details.

Suddenly the air raid alarm sounded. Brausig calmly kept on typing. Dushek paced around the table one more time, stopped in front of me and said in a sepulchral voice:"Are you afraid?"

How was I supposed to answer? I had been threatened with a beating and it would have been ridiculous to say that I wasn't frightened of that. So I said nothing. Three more times around the table and Dushek stopped in front of me again and repeated: "Are you afraid?"

I lowered my eyes. Suddenly his colleague looked up and smiled. "She's not afraid of the air raid, that's the least of her worries."

At that moment I understood for the first time, that this big broad shouldered fellow was shaking with fear. The notion that in this situation I would be afraid of an air raid on Paris seemed so funny to me that I burst out laughing. Brausig laughed with me and the whole thing became farcical. The interrogation was concluded quickly and the prison van brought me back to Fresnes.

Marthe and I were always trying to outwit the Gretchens and we took some chances in doing so. Once we were brought an enormous pile of worn – out men's socks and told to darn them. We each got about twenty pairs. We could see that they had been worn through and torn in the course of a great many marches. As always, the French women were full of zeal to darn the holes as skillfully as possible. Marthe too proved her mastery of needle and thread.

Handiwork had always been my weak side; I usually got the lowest grade in that subject. In Toulouse, the first time I had to spend a semester break apart from my husband, I tried to knit him a pullover. All my friends gave me advice. Despite that, the neckline came out so small, that not even Jascha's narrow head could pass through it. I cut the upper part off and tried to make a turtle neck, but then it came out looking like a medium sized cartwheel and with all the love in the world Jascha only wore it twice.

I darned a couple of small holes as well as I could. When I took up the next stocking, I found a giant hole staring at me. That was just too stupid for me. I took a double strand of wool yarn and simply pulled the edges of the hole together. Marthe looked at me pityingly several times; then she jumped up and said, laughing, this was really a great idea; this was a way to make the socks unusable. The other two women in the cell were afraid, but Marthe went to work with zest. When we gave the stockings back, the ones our cellmates had mended correctly were on top. But then the guard pulled out one of my creations. She was speechless and when she had several of the socks in her hand, which looked like unsuccessful washrags, she went on a rampage. We were locked in a dark cell for several hours, while the Gretchens looked through every bag, every straw sack, every soap box, threw everything onto the floor and tore everything up. The only thing they didn't find was a copy of my verses that one of the women had made. They were standing on a note that was visibly sticking out of her coat pocket. Once again my good star protected me from worse things.

One day a very well-dressed lady, aged forty-five to fifty, appeared in our cell. She had a suitcase with her, which was very unusual. In general, people being arrested were not allowed any time to pack things. To judge by her appearance, this woman had not suffered from the general shortage of food and cosmetics.

With an energetic voice, she laid claim to the only bed in the cell. When she began talking to us, Marthe and I were very guarded. Turning her well-defined profile to us, in which the big nose and the rather protruding lips stood out, she asked: "Can't you see, which family I come from?"

We looked at her blankly and shook our heads.

"The blood of the Bourbons flows in my veins. I am related to the Comte de Paris, descendant of the last ruling King of France!"

Seeing that we were unimpressed by this information, her face took on an offended expression.

During the eight days that she spent in our cell she got two packages, an unheard of privilege. Nevertheless she complained bitterly about conditions in Fresnes. "My husband had it so much better as a political prisoner in a French prison! Radio, newspapers, books, his own bed sheets! I could bring him food every day. He got visits and letters twice a week. We didn't know how good we had it!"

The following facts came out: The husband of our blue-blooded fellow prisoner had been, in 1936, one of the leaders of a secret Fascist organization in France. As in the American Ku Klux Klan, the members had worn a black hood, the "cagoule". They called themselves "Cagoulards" after the hood.

After the bestial murder of the Italian anti-Fascists Roselli, the ringleaders had finally been locked up and some of them stayed in prison until May 1940. Most of them had already been released in 1939, at the beginning of the war. Many of the French officers had ties with the Cagoulards and Weygand, the chief of the general staff, intervened personally on their behalf.

The husband of our lady was thus free and a number of his former friends were sitting in the government of Marshal Petain. Another Fascist, with whom the Cagoulards had collaborated, was Jacques Doriot, collaborator number one. He not only turned French workers over to the German occupiers; in 1941 he also founded the so-called Légion Française, which fought for Hitler in the Soviet Union.

In 1940, Doriot and his allies had already turned to the Cagoulards and invited them to collaborate with the "victor". Most of them agreed. Doriot also repeatedly asked the husband of our lady to support the "Légion Française". But, while he was ready to fight against the Communists, he refused to fight along-side the Germans.

Now, in spring 1944, Doriot had approached her husband once again and, once again, he refused. By this time, almost all the French had come to hate the supporters of Hitler and people could see which side was going to win.

The couple was taken into custody and spent about ten days in the prison at Fresnes, days that Marthe and I spent in endless, perhaps not entirely fruitless discussions.

Shortly after my interrogation in Avenue Foche, Jean wrote me a message on the window: "Etienne sends greetings. No comment."

From this I drew the conclusion that Etienne had received my message, "The photographer's wife does not know Etienne," and I felt somewhat calmer. Then, in the middle of May, I was taken to interrogation again.

Before we climbed into the prison van, we were lined up in the courtyard and counted. The head count, here as in the concentration camps, where it became a cruel torture, was the Nazis' most important and most sacred procedure. At the last moment two more men in handcuffs and ankle chains were shoved into the van. Their faces bore the marks of very brutal beatings by the Gestapo. Someone whispered, "Two English paratroopers; they got caught in Normandy."

While we were being unloaded in Avenue Foche, the scene in the reception area was rather confused. I made use of this to place myself next to the Englishmen and to slip some bread and sugar to them, something that the women prisoners always carried and whispered, in English: "Things are all right, the preparations for the landings are nearly finished." At this moment a tall, white-haired man leaned over the stairway landing and called out:

"Schlesinger-Segal to interrogation!" I climbed the stairs slowly, looking anxiously at the elderly man in police uniform, who made a somewhat athletic impression without seeming too rigidly military.

"What did you have to say to that man down there and what did you pass him?"

I don't know, even today, why I answered in Berlin dialect. Maybe I recognized a fellow Berliner in this interrogator. "I cheered the poor guy up a little. You messed him up pretty bad. And I slipped him a bit of bread."

"You seem to have too much to eat," he said in a not unfriendly way. "Are you a Berliner? Schlesinger?" he looked in his file folder. "Was your father Dr. Arthur Schlesinger and did he have a clinic in Koeniggraetz Strasse?"

I nodded.

"What happened to him?"

"On April 1, 1933, when he was subjected to the boycott on Jewish businesses, despite his officer's rank and his medals, he committed suicide. An SS man seated at the next desk looked up. Why had my father killed himself in 1933, he wanted to know. Things weren't so bad for the Jews then. I explained to both of them, that one did not need to wait for the worst to happen. One could draw the obvious conclusion without that. At this point a long discussion about the Jewish question ensued.

Suddenly the inspector told me, that I had to admit that there was a great difference between me as a German Jewish woman and the eastern Jews and that I could not be equated to the Polish Jews.

"That is exactly what we Marxists say: it is not a question of race, but rather culture, education and living conditions are the decisive factors," I answered, without considering where I was. But the SS man just shrugged his shoulders and the inspector ordered: "Enough discussion."

He showed me several photos. I only recognized two faces; one of them was Etienne. I shook my head. He pointed to Etienne. "You don't know him?"

Again I denied it.

"So and what does 'The photographer's wife does not know Etienne.' mean?"

He stood up, went to his filing cabinet and rummaged around in it. The file folder with Etienne's statement was lying open on the desk. I could see, that he had admitted some things, but not a word about our technical section or about Jascha's work.

Etienne's statement fit in very well with what I had put together. As soon as the inspector sat down again, I began to tell my little story: Normally I would have had nothing to do with Etienne. I only knew him by accident, a little flirtation, he was an exceptionally charming young guy. Last summer he had asked me to do him a favor. Someone had written two leaflets in Cyrillic script on a typewriter. The leaflets were intended for the Russian prisoners in the camps at the Atlantic Wall. If they were mimeographed they would be too large to be smuggled into the camps. He had heard that one of my acquaintances was a very good photographer; perhaps he could make about twenty readable copies. I had met with Etienne three times in regard to the matter and then we had gone out to eat together.

The inspector asked me for some details. He accepted my explanation that I had done everything merely out of friendship for Etienne. The interrogation was ended. He escorted me back to the prison van. As we were standing in front of the elevator, the door opened and out came Duschek, the Viennese giant who always made me tremble.

"You impudent little liar!" he said and lunged at me. My "Berliner friend" pulled me back and giving me a shove that sent me stumbling into the elevator, stood in front of me and tried to calm Duschek down. "It's not important, just a few details." We rode down. Before he turned me over to the guards, he said softly, "I know you're lying, but I'll bring Etienne in and I'll get everything I want to know out of him."

Certainly I have too often let my instincts guide me, but in most cases things turned out well and here I had nothing left to lose.

I looked at him pleadingly and said, "That's not at all nice of you. There's nothing in this business to incriminate Etienne. If he kept quiet, it's only because he's a gentleman and didn't want to drag me into it. You can't pin that on him – blame me."

During the next few days I woke up every morning bathed in sweat, thinking: How's Etienne? What have they found out?

Once again it was Jean, my unknown correspondent, who laid my fears to rest. "Greetings from Etienne, everything's all right," was the brief message one morning.

That whole day, I never left the window. When twilight came, Jean began again: The inspector left your file open on his desk. Etienne was able to repeat the entire story. The inspector told him that he wouldn't believe a word either of you said, but when Etienne insisted he didn't know your husband, he was satisfied.

A short time later Jean sent the message that Etienne had been sent on a transport. He was sent to Neuengamme. The prisoners at the camp at Neuengamme were taken to Luebeck at the beginning of March 1945 and loaded onto ships, in which the SS wanted to escape to Denmark. The ships were bombed during an attack on shipping in Luebeck Bay. Etienne drowned with several thousand comrades.

We learned about the Allied landing in Normandy on the day it happened, June 6, 1944. The frantic guards were not able to silence "Radio Fresnes".

The transports were speeded up at the end of June. The Germans wanted to empty the prisons before Paris was liberated. Marthe and her brother Jean were taken away on a transport.

CHAPTER XI

1944

Life in Auschwitz – Annie

"Somewhere on the horizon, clouds of smoke rose up to the sky."

My hour struck at the end of June. I was taken to Drancy. Beginning at the end of 1941 more than eighty thousand Jews were deported from Drancy to undisclosed destinations. Most of the members of my resistance group were transported to the east by way of Drancy.

Frederike had been scheduled for deportation at the end of August 1944 and, fortunately, liberated while she was still in Paris. Of the men in my group the only survivor was the husband of my comrade Anni, the Viennese painter Professor Heinrich Sussman. When Soviet troops approached the camp at Auschwitz at the beginning of 1945, most of the prisoners were evacuated to Mauthausen near Vienna. There, by order of the Gestapo, our comrades were bestially killed on April 17th 1945. Heinrich Sussman had announced that he would never survive the transport, he was too old and too undernourished to endure it. He hid in the typhoid barracks, in the same bed with a typhoid patient. The SS avoided entering this block; they were afraid of infection. In the bed of the sick man, Heinrich Sussman was safe from infection. He did not become infected. On January 21, 1945 he was liberated by the Red Army and in May 1945 he returned to

France on a ship, by way of Odessa. There he found his wife again, whom he had thought dead.

When I was taken to Drancy the camp was filled to capacity. A transport was being prepared for the east. There were three hundred children, who had been discovered in a Jewish orphanage; there were men and women, teen-agers, very old men in wheel chairs, and invalids carried on stretchers.

Since 1941, not a single sign of life had been received in Paris from people who had been taken away on transports. Despite this fact, only very few of those now waiting in Drancy understood what deportation really meant for them. On my very first day at Drancy I made contact with a young German émigré woman, a born Rothschild, married to a German comrade who was with the Macquis after having escaped from the camp at Le Vernet.

Although she was married to an "Aryan", she and her eleven year old daughter had been interned in Drancy but not, until now, deported. Now, shortly before the transport, the quota of prisoners had not quite been achieved and the ranks were being filled with spouses from mixed marriages and, for the first time, with half-Aryans. The young woman was summoned to the commandant of Drancy. He told her that to his regret she was going with the transport. However, he allowed her to choose whether her daughter should go with her or not. I tried during two nights to persuade her to leave the child behind. The English and French were only a hundred kilometers from Paris. (The camp was liberated twenty days later.) The father or some organization would take care of the little girl. But she didn't want to believe me. "As long as I can be together with my child I can protect her. I'll do everything to help her." Together with her daughter and three hundred orphaned children she was transported in separate freight cars. All the occupants of these cars were sent directly to the gas chamber upon arrival at Auschwitz.

A freight car with young men was specially sealed and guarded. The other freight cars held old people, teen-agers and families. For each freight car, the head of a family was chosen and told that he would be responsible for everything that happened during the transport. If someone escaped from his area, he, his wife and his children would bear the consequences. Our freight car leader guarded us better than the German guards did.

The four days in the cattle car fitted with bars, together with seventy-five people in the high temperatures of summer, cannot be described.

That no one either to the left or right of our long travel route took note of this transport from Hell, is more than improbable. On the third day both of our two daily buckets of water had been used up. We stopped at a little station. Some elderly soldiers in field-grey uniforms, who were part of our escort, had opened the car doors during the trip and had not closed them when the train stopped. Two men in the car next to ours jumped off with their buckets and got water from a nearby tap. During ten months of arrest I had learned to make use of every opportunity. I grabbed a bucket and jumped down, followed by an elderly man. Just as I was coming back with my bucket, an officer came running along the platform, yelling. I climbed back into the cattle car as quickly as I could. The officer knocked the bucket out of the hand of our second water carrier, but we were able to pull him in quickly and close the door. The yelling continued. Apparently he had caught some other unfortunates. Suddenly he came back to our car, went up to the grey-haired guard and slapped him on each cheek. "Let the Jews die!"

As the train moved out, the soldier crouched on the footboard, wiping the sweat from his brow. An old, tired man. I bent down to him and said, "I am ashamed to be the daughter of a German officer. It's good that my father is dead."

He looked up at me sadly and whispered: "I'm ashamed too, but what should I do?"

Arrival at Auschwitz has been described by others; more completely and better than I am able to do. After the hell of the cattle cars we could breathe the cool night air. And then everything went so rapidly that, fortunately, we didn't grasp what was going on. Someone called out: "Old people and women with children to the right, women to the left." SS men stood on the platform and pushed us forward with their rifle butts. For the first time we heard the commands that would accompany us throughout our entire time in the camps: "Move! Move! Faster! Stay in line!" Stumbling, we pressed forward, into the glare of the spotlight, past an elegant, tall, dark-haired officer, who poked at the marchers with the butt of his whip, directing them to the group of the old people and children, or to the other side. Dr. Mengele! He was whistling, quite audibly, a melody from Wagner's Goetterdaemmerung. Once he stopped whistling, when a couple of women began to weep and cry out: "My mother! I want to stay with my mother! My sister! You can't take the children away!" He landed two or three blows with his whip and shouted in a loud, commanding voice: "Quiet there! Or something's going to happen!" Then he went on with the selection. Most of the people in our transport, including the three hundred children from the orphanage, were gassed.

There were about one hundred and sixty women left. At thirty-one I was one of the oldest among them. We were led by the SS men past the watchtowers to the disinfection station. Some of the younger girls could speak Yiddish and thus understood a little German. They kept asking the guards: "Where are our parents going? Where are they taking our relatives?" The SS guards shrugged their shoulders. Some of them answered: "To a camp for sick people and children where they won't have to work." In an enormous hall we were ordered: "Take everything off, right down to the shoes." Someone, I believe they were prisoners, tore he last pieces of underwear from our bodies and took all our jewelry. Because my wedding ring wouldn't come off my finger, an SS man simply cut it off with a pincers, together with a piece of skin.

In less than an hour we had all been shorn completely bald. We first got a hot shower, then a cold one; then we found ourselves in a huge room without windows. There stood the little Parisiennes, who had once looked so pretty, naked and trembling from the cold, with their ghastly shorn heads and the SS men stood in the hallway and the doors and eyed them contemptuously. Three or four of the girls began to weep. Others called out: "Pst! Don't cry. Do you want to do these pigs a favor and blubber in front of them?"

"Bravo," someone standing next to me said in German. "At least they've got some sense." It was a woman of the same age as myself, well grown with large black eyes, high cheekbones and very pale. Her face, despite the disfiguring nakedness of her skull, retained its attractiveness. That was how I came to know Anni Sussman, a Viennese who , just like me, had been arrested for resisting the German army, together with her husband. She too had been taken from Fresnes to Drancy in the last days of July. We were taken to Birkenau B II, one of the quarantine camps intended for Jews assigned to work, within the Auschwitz complex. This may have been because we were only a few political prisoners, or perhaps at that point a state of confusion prevailed: for example Anni's name and my name are not on the list of those deported on July 31, 1944. On the registers discovered later, the last number is A 16795. However, I bear the number A 16808 and my comrade Anni bears the number A 16809.

It was August 1944 and at Auschwitz they could no longer afford the luxury of simply destroying labor power.

A progressive selection took place. The first selection was carried out when prisoners were delivered and then again, two or three months later, when those among the survivors who were less abl to resist the terror of the guards, the hunger and the fear, had been reduced to walking skeletons. Those who were still usable as labor were sent on new transports to Germany, while the unusable were sent to the gas chamber and to the incinerator. The Red Army was less than two hundred kilometers away and even here in the camp something had changed.

As strange as it seems, we did not wear prison garb. Only the old prisoners wore the blue stripes. At the disinfection station pieces of clothing which had been taken from earlier arrivals were thrown at us. Tall women got silk summer dresses which didn't reach their knees and short stout girls got jerseys that dragged on the ground and whose upper portion couldn't even be buttoned up. I got a pink wool dress that reached to my ankles. It was shortened and the material that was cut away was used to make me a brassiere. When my shoes were stolen a week later, because I had forgotten to take them with me when I lay down on the plank bed, the girls sewed me a pair of slippers out of some pieces of blanket.

But no matter how hard we tried, we still presented a shocking appearance. After only a few days, in the dress in which we slept and sat on the ground, often without water or soap, we looked totally ragged. Added to this the shaven heads, which had been burned by the scorching sun of August, because the sensitive skin of the head was unprotected and it was strictly forbidden to cover the head with a piece of cloth or paper bandage.

These motley figures, whose dresses, of course, were very soon covered with a layer of grey dust, looked like something out of a horror movie. As far as the eye could see, yellow-grey clay, yellow-brown wooden barracks and the barbed wire which surrounded our camp with its 20,000 women and all the neighboring camps. High watchtowers everywhere, from which the machine guns of the SS men were trained upon us. Not a blade of grass, not a shrub, not a tree, not a butterfly, not a caterpillar anywhere. Not even a crow flew overhead. Somewhere on the horizon, clouds of smoke rose up to the sky. The female guards and the prisoners serving as camp police, the "Kapos", never failed to remind us of the smoke, with the threat: "If you filthy French women don't follow orders and behave yourselves, you'll go to the gas oven too."

Dirty or nasty French women – it's certainly true that in France I had often been the object of discrimination as a foreigner. But here in Auschwitz I was suddenly a dirty French woman and for that reason alone in solidarity with my comrades. We had been crammed on purpose into a block of barracks with several hundred Hungarian and Polish women. What that meant, first of all, was that they had even less space on their plank beds and fewer blankets. If, until now, two out of three of them had had their own bowls to eat from, now it was only every second one who could claim this privilege for herself. We, on the other hand, slurped down our soup from a common bowl, without spoons, in groups of three or four. For the most part, we were only able to communicate by means of a few fragments of "camp German" that every prisoner quickly learned, out of self preservation, after being beaten by the Germans. On one of the first evenings I was the last one to return to the barracks. As I came in, the block leader and her helpers had just begun an inspection.

If they had found me in the corridor, a sound thrashing would have been the least punishment I could expect. I tried to squeeze into one of the plank beds. In vain. Polish curses. I tried on the other side of the room. Hungarian curses. Finally, when I said something in German, people made room for me on a plank and asked if I were German or French.

This system, of inciting the different groups of prisoners against each other and using one group to oppress or even destroy the others, was the diabolical element in the German machinery of destruction: "divide et impera", the motto of the Roman Empire. On every occasion when something was taken away or a punishment was announced, or an especially harsh order was given, a comment would be made, putting the blame on some other national group. As a matter of principle, criminals were assigned to act as Kapos and block leaders overseeing the political prisoners. Non-political prisoners were supervised by Kapos and block leaders of some other nationality. The terrible thing was that the more the prisoners were oppressed, the more they were tortured, the easier it was to misuse many of them, especially if they came from semi-feudal and semi-Fascist countries. The Hungarian women who were deported to Birkenau in 1944 came from rural areas, primarily from villages on the Romanian border. Only very young girls had survived the many selections. Most of them had no understanding at all of what was happening. They only spoke Hungarian, so that we were unable to communicate with them. In August 1944, in the quarantine camp in Birkenau, there was, with the exception of two women doctors, not a single living Czech Jewish woman. According to what I was told, the Czech women were unsuited for any kind of forced labor and were sent directly to the gas chamber.

At this point in time, some of the overseer positions in the Birkenau camps were held by Slovakian prisoners, who spoke Hungarian, a little German and of course Slovak. They were all quite young, between seventeen and twenty years of age. Relatively strong, pretty, coming mostly from a religious environment, they had been through it all. They had been taken from their families while they were still almost children, or their relatives had been beaten to death before their eyes. Only those who endured the hardest labor, hunger, frost, typhoid and constant tortures got one of these positions. The strongest survived and those who somehow managed to adjust. The system was so ingeniously contrived, that any violation of the rules, any lack of discipline in the block, resulted not only in harsh punishments for the block leader, but could also mean the death of many women. The SS always stood in the background, ready to strike. After two or three years, these block leaders no longer knew that they were nothing but the watchdogs of the Nazis and that their obedience only served a seamless process of destruction.

Three days after our arrival the following scene was played out: In our group there was a French woman who had worked as a manager at Lanvin, one of the most important Parisian fashion houses. When she arrived, she drew attention to herself, not only because of her height of almost 1.80 meters, or about 5' 8", but also because of her elegance. After she had been handed a grey dress, much too short and much too wide for her, she looked, with her bald head and her snow white face and little grey eyes, like a scarecrow. The only things she had left were her sandals, which revealed her toes in the most tasteful sort of way. As a Lanvin employee she had access to the most modern, highest quality nail polish and her toenails shone a lustrous red.

Because of her height she always stood in the back row, so as not to attract too much attention. On this morning the young Slovakian block leader happened to inspect the rear ranks. She suddenly noticed the painted toenails of the fashion stylist. She began to rage like a madwoman and with her stick she beat the trembling victim until she lay motionless on the floor. "You French devils, you whores, you sluts. Fingernails painted red! Toenails painted red! You're going to work till your nails break. Just like us, we who had to shovel coal with our bare hands. You French bitches, all you ever thought about was clothes and makeup. You lived the good life while your sisters burned. You didn't care about what happened to us, about our suffering and our tears. Now it's your turn! You don't know how good you've got it! You don't know what we've suffered!" With tears in her eyes she scrutinized us. None of the French women wept. In most of the faces she could only read revulsion and hatred. "All right. The whole block, kneel! Arms above your heads!" That was a favorite punishment. Kneeling on the hard clay, with raised arms, quickly became a terrible torture in the scorching sun.

She walked down the rows and handed out blows to anyone whose attitude displeased her. Then she went back to the front and turned to the Hungarian and Polish women:"If you have to kneel down here, you can thank the French women for it. If the

French and Dutch women don't keep order in the block, you'll get punished with them!"

This destroyed any possibility of solidarity between us and the Hungarians. We got along somewhat better with the Polish prisoners. They had had some contact to resistance fighters, or they knew of relatives who belonged to the workers' movement in the western countries. In addition, there was the unshakable principle of the Polish Jews: One may never strike or torture another human being.

Although the national and linguistic differences led to harsh antagonisms, in Auschwitz the social function of the famous Jewish sense of family became clear to me. (Among Jews from the highly developed industrial countries this sense of family had, however, already been lost.) Much later, a scene from "Fiddler on the Roof" reminded me of my experiences in Auschwitz. Tevje and all the Jewish families are being expelled from the village. Tevje asks the butcher: "Where are you going to go?"

"To my brother in America; he can't stand me and he'll be angry when he has to take me in."

Tevje, too, wants to go to a cousin with whom he is on hostile terms.

We had been in the camp a few days, when one evening some Polish and Ukrainian girls came sneaking into the block. They were wearing headscarves and blue-white clothing and we knew at once that they were longtime prisoners who had fixed work assignments in the camp. "The camp bourgeoisie", as we called them. They spoke mostly Yiddish or broken German. Due to my meager knowledge of Swiss German I understood some Yiddish and also their German, so I was called on to interpret.

I translated the question, whether anyone here was from Suvalki. A young girl spoke out and said her father came from there.

When she gave her name, she was asked if she was the daughter of so and so, who had emigrated to Paris in 1920. She said she was.

A little Polish woman came up to her and hugged her and had me tell our French woman, who had no idea what was happening, that her father was the youngest brother of the Polish woman's father and that they were blood relations and cousins. "Listen, I work in the kitchen, we need another hand. Report tomorrow after roll call to Franka – tell her you're my cousin; that's how you can get through this."

This family research had positive results in other cases. A girl found her aunt. The young French woman had hurt her shoulder and the wound began to fester. Getting it disinfected was out of the question. Her aunt brought her salve and bandages. The girl was saved.

We had still another weapon: the solidarity and moral strength of the political prisoners. There were only a very few of us who had done illegal work, only six or seven with the two Austrian women and me. There were also some eighteen and twenty year old Parisiennes whose brothers and fathers belonged to leftist organizations. These girls were helpful in certain difficult situations and showed interest and understanding for political questions. Once again the first contacts were established through the medium of songs. The Marseillaise, songs of the Paris Commune, "When the cherries are ripe the Republic calls on us"; "The Soldiers of the Moor"; "My blond girl, do you hear the call of Great Lenin in the street?" The French partisan song: "Friends, do you hear the cry of the ravens in the field?"; a fighting song of the Young Communists: "We were three comrades and marched hand in hand" and also my "poem" from Fresnes: "Don't let yourselves be frightened. For there are far worse things."

After a few days almost all the French women sang when we loafed around for hours between the barracks. "How can you sing, especially such happy songs? Aren't you afraid?" the Polish and Hungarian women asked us, while the Dutch women tried to sing along.

And when we even formed a circle and danced, they started to cry. "This is going to turn out bad; the Germans are going to punish you and us both. The Kapos have already been complaining about the smart-mouthed, trifling French women." The camp administration grasped very quickly that these musical demonstrations gave us strength and courage. Our songs were a defense against total enslavement. After we had been fourteen days in Birkenau, an order came down from the camp administration, which was passed on to us by the block leaders with spiteful glee: From now on only German songs could be sung – singing in other languages was strictly forbidden.

I was always among the most active in discussions and not even blows could silence my smart mouth or stop me from trying to make contacts. But Anni Sussmann quickly became the intellectual leader of our little group. She not only had the most political experience of any of us; she also had qualities that I lacked: judgment and caution. Even in Auschwitz I continued to be guided by my temperament and my feelings, but Anni Sussmann analyzed the situation with a precise and critical gaze.

Our group very quickly reached an agreement. Certainly there were gas ovens. There was also no doubt, that selections were constantly taking place in the camp. Anni had witnessed one such in the sick block, in which, on orders from the SS doctor, selected sick prisoners who were still alive were taken away in the same truck with the corpses. Indeed, some of the unfortunate patients were lying underneath the corpses. But to keep the young girls, who had been separated from their families, from falling into utter despair, we had to convince them that there were no gas ovens here, that their aging parents and brothers and sisters had been taken to another camp where conditions were not so harsh.

In fact, during August and September 1944 smaller transports began to arrive from the east. These transports had been dispatched without a prior selection: perhaps because a selection was not considered worth the trouble, or perhaps because no preparations had been made for one. And so there were now old people and children in Birkenau. The Hungarian and Polish women had constantly warned us "Don't go to the doctor, you'll end up in the gas oven." But we were able to establish that many women returned from the sick block to the barracks after a few days. We exaggerated these facts in order to pretend to many of the young French women that, while there were gas ovens, they were used to incinerate the bodies of the dead and infected straw. The gassing of living people, we told them, was a lie told by the block leaders and the Kapos, intended to demoralize us.

By the summer of 1944 a great number of the Jewish women from bourgeois-democratic countries had lived underground before being arrested and had experienced the solidarity of the resistance movement. They had confidence in the victory of the Allies. Women from the semi-Fascist and backward countries on the other hand had experienced every kind of horror and torture. No one had helped them against the murderers and they no longer believed in the possibility of resistance.

While some Slovakian women held leadership positions among the prisoners, the SS had filled the subordinate positions in the transit camp at Birkenau with Hungarian women. They were the "Stubovas" who had to keep the block and the camp facilities clean and orderly. For this purpose they had been issued brooms, whose handles they used to secure respect and space for themselves.

Sometimes they were also armed with a stick, which they used to herd us from one place to another, or, on orders from on high, block our access to the washroom or to water. We immediately dubbed these Stubovas the "lackeys of the camp bourgeoisie". The situation was made more acute by the fact that they really could communicate only with their sticks.

Once the block leader called us all together, had everyone kneel down and addressed us as follows: "One of the Kapos whacked one of these damned French women with her stick and she had it coming to her. And that piece of crap had the nerve to slap the Kapo's face. One of the German bosses showed her what discipline means in this camp and now she's in the sick block and she's not coming back. And now you're going to see what happens to you. You don't know what order and obedience means. Since the French and Belgians and Dutch got here, there's no more discipline!"

This speech had the intended success with some of the women. Some prayed, others began to wail. "How could she do that, now we'll all be punished. They'll send her to the gas for sure."

We French women were of course affected by this. We discussed it: how we would be punished and what would happen to the unlucky woman. Many of the group stated that no matter what happened, she had done the right thing. At last there was one of us who showed courage and defended herself. The lamentations stopped when nothing more happened. When the woman who had been beaten returned after five days, pale but self-confident, we felt triumphant.

Anni became our main problem child. She was five months pregnant on her arrival in Auschwitz. At the beginning of September her condition was clearly visible when she was naked. Anni knew that pregnant women were either selected to be killed or, what was still worse, taken to the A block where medical experiments were performed on them.

When we had to stand in formation she always found a place in the rear ranks. At the end of September, shortly after morning roll call, the labor pains began, much too soon. We were able to get Anni back to the block without attracting attention. The first problem was to find a suitable bed in a dark corner where the bit of straw wasn't too filthy. No one had a rag or a piece of paper to wipe off the bed.

Elisa, the youngest, was sent out to try to fetch a bowl of water. But the washroom barracks, the only place where there was water, was guarded by two Stubovas with clubs. They chased Elisa away. But she did see a freshly washed blanket hanging on a line and grabbed it when she ran past. She was able to bring it back to the block. Things were happening very quickly. The child was lying in a puddle on the wooden planks. Rosi the room orderly held it up and called out: "Anni, it's a boy!"

A high loud voice said: "Can't somebody find a scissors or a knife? We've got to cut the umbilical cord, or at least a string to tie if off with?"

Rosi ran out and came back with half a bread ration. Another woman, who seemed to have connections, was dispatched with the admonition to trade it for a strong, clean string. She came back in a few minutes with twine that looked clean. The cord was cut and tied with lightning speed. And now the real problem began – how to get Anni into the sick block? She couldn't walk. Not only was she too weak, but a prisoner who encountered one of the overseers and didn't stand at attention, risked being beaten half to death on the spot.

We wrapped Anni in the stolen blanket and four of us carried her with all possible speed to the sick barracks. Just like moving a corpse in a gangster movie.

I don't know how the Jewish doctors managed to conceal Anni from the SS doctor on duty. Dr. Fenniger, a woman physician, did everything she could to secure a bed for her. Unfortunately she was unable to do much more. There were no gynecological instruments in the camp. Anyone needing surgery was unfit for work and belonged in the gas oven. Mengele took children away at once. He had only one treatment for infants: a phenol injection in the heart.

The doctor was not even able to boil water, in order to do a real cleanup. Anni was washed off with cold water, mixed with permanganate and the afterbirth was removed. We had little hope of ever seeing the totally exhausted sick woman again, especially when we learned, a couple of days later, that Anni had dysentery and a fever. I believe it is really due to the efforts and courage of Dr. Fenniger, that Anni returned to the block a few days later, terribly pale and weak but still alive.

Health inspections in the camp consisted in having us strip off naked to be checked for lice and above all for scabies. Eruptions were found among a large number of women, which were always very quickly identified as measles, or symptomatic of scarlet fever. The sick women were brought to an infection barracks, where it was known that Mengele personally held regular selections.

At the beginning of October I caught measles. I didn't know whether I had already had this illness as a child. The infection barracks was so overfilled that I was put in a bed already occupied by a thirteen year old girl. She had arrived in a transport containing between a hundred and fifty and two hundred people from a Polish labor camp. Holding a selection there was not considered worth the expense.

Since the girl also had measles, we were given a common blanket and a common bowl. In fact, we both ate with the same wooden spoon, carved in the camp, a gift of our Parisiennes.

By camp standards I was robust and husky, so there was only one way for us to share a bed. We lay head to foot: my feet next to her head and her feet next to my shoulders. The doctors were helpless. They diagnosed the illnesses, swabbed the throats of the patients, filled the hot water bottles with herbal tea in order to use them instead of compresses and distributed the last of the medications that the Hungarian women had brought with them, as well as they could. There was no hot water and there were no instruments of any kind.

Although there were many cases of childhood diseases, which are dreaded when they occur among adults, there were no complications. The real threat came from the regular inspections by the SS doctors who sent every patient, who was too thin and who could not stand at attention, or who did not climb out of bed quickly enough, to the special ward – practically a death sentence.

The doctor was shocked at my high fever and at the swelling of the glands in my neck, which was so pronounced that she thought it might be mumps. She recommended a high fluid intake. But since there was absolutely no water and in the mornings we only got some tea in our common bowl, that seemed a useless suggestion.

Here I was helped by my absolute lack of prejudice in regard to food and drink. During the day I simply drank the one and a half liters of the brew with which our hot water bottles had been filled. The others watched me in horror. Only an Italian Jewish woman, daughter of a well-known German professor in Florence, who had been arrested for political reasons, followed my example. She too survived.

The success of this method was that the fever, which during the first three evenings had risen to 40.5 and 41 degrees Celsius, went down on the fourth morning to 37.5 and after five days the evening temperatures remained at 37.5.

On the fourth day it became apparent that the little girl whose bed I was sharing had diphtheria. This time I was certain that I had never had this illness. There was no single bed available, but I got my own blanket and my own bowl. We continued using the same spoon, but I did not become infected. On the sixth day I was free of fever and returned to the barracks. That same evening I stood up for four and a half hours at roll call, in a cold wind.

In discussions with doctors who had personal experience of the prisons and camps, one thing repeatedly becomes clear: in the completely abnormal health conditions, all the normal medical and biological rules ceased to apply to the undernourished, weakened and terrorized prisoners. In many cases, doctors and nurses were able to save prisoners whose conditions were thought terminal, either through radical measures, or the correct and careful administration of the few medications available, or through psychological influence. Many doctors and nurses among the prisoners performed true medical miracles thanks to their courage and ability.

On the other hand it is all the more worthy of condemnation, that in a civilized country, which Germany after all had once been, trained physicians could carry out such diabolical and scientifically stupid and useless experiments on living human beings. Using the excuse of medical and biological experimentation, Nazi doctors, in cooperation with a number of medical and scientific institutions, tortured thousands and thousands of prisoners to death. In seventy books and almost as many articles on the problems of such experiments, I have not found a single case, in which a concrete medical result was achieved.

At the Nuremberg trials the attorneys for the murderers in white coats offered as a defense, that in the history of medicine reports have been made from time to time about dangerous experiments performed on voluntary subjects, who were, however, mainly criminals. Thanks to these human experiments the causes of some diseases were discovered and cures were found for others.

At the reserve military hospital Hamburg-Wandsbek V the internist Dr. Heinrich Bernig chose a group of Soviet prisoners of war among whom nutritional edemas and intestinal inflammations were especially advanced. He injected them with vitamin B 1 and other medicines, in order to ascertain whether this treatment would have any effect on the consequences of hunger – without any success whatever. All the prisoners on whom this experiment was performed died. A result that any internist would have been able to predict.

At Strutthof and especially at Dachau so-called terminal experiments were carried out. Men were submerged in ice water, in order to determine at what point they would freeze. Others were exposed to low pressure conditions without oxygen masks equivalent to 1200 meters of altitude. At a conference of military medical consultants in December 1942 in Berlin these experiments were described in a report. The report did not however make clear the number of deaths. Some of the doctors who were present later claimed that they had rejected these experiments, but none of the ninety-five participants stated his reservations publicly.

Thousands of prisoners were mutilated and tortured in pseudo-medical experiments in order to simplify and accelerate the technology of the destruction of human life. Russians, Poles and Czechs were supposed to work for the German army, of course, but their ability to reproduce had been destroyed. The gynecologist Professor Clauberg had young Jewish girls delivered to his experimental project "Negative Population Policy". He rented them from the camp commandant at Dachau for one mark per week. Most of them died during the experiments from lack of care.

In July 1944, Clauberg wrote to Professor Karl Brandt, the Reich Commissioner for Hygiene and Health. "The method which I have developed is practically complete. If the tests continue to yield the same results, a physician working in an appropriately equipped facility, assisted by a staff of 10, will be able to sterilize several hundred, or perhaps even 1000 persons in one day."

The Auschwitz doctor Mengele, who usually reserved the selection for the gas chambers for himself, as a personal privilege, specialized in experiments on twins and investigated certain hereditary malformations. He worked at Auschwitz on behalf of the Director of the Kaiser Wilhelm Institute for Anthropology, Professor Otmar BaronVerschuer. Organ specimens taken from the people whom Mengele had killed were forwarded as urgent military shipments to the Institute for Racial Biology and Anthropological Research in Berlin and their receipt was duly acknowledged

In the course of a discussion about Mengele, Professor Karl Gottschaldt, who was then an assistant at the Kaiser Wilhelm Institute, told me that, at the institute, glass jars containing specimen human eyes which exhibited anomalous coloring were on display for anyone to see. These eyes had been taken from a Gypsy clan, in which this peculiarity was hereditary. The labels on the jars indicated that all the members of the clan, from infants to aged elders, had died within forty-eight hours.

While only two hundred to three hundred SS doctors directly participated in torture and murder, the circle of persons who knew about the killing of human beings, about "elimination through labor" and about the use of human beings as experimental animals, included a great many more.

During the years 1941 through 1944 the IG Farben and Bayer companies tested their medications on prisoners who had been previously infected with spotted typhus, hepatitis, tuberculosis and boils. Most of the medications showed little or no effect. Carl Ludwig Lautenschlaeger, the works manager of the pharmaceutical firm Hoechst, stated before the court at Nuremberg, that he had stopped the delivery of medications to Auschwitz after learning of the human experiments, "especially since he regarded such experiments as worthless, from the standpoint of immunology." But it is certain that these experiments were performed right up to the end.

In a letter to the commandant of Auschwitz, the works manager of IG Farben stated that the women who had been delivered to them at two hundred marks "per unit" were unusable. Due to their nutritional condition, they would not be able to survive hormonal experiments. The Bayer company on the other hand confirmed the receipt of prisoners – at one hundred seventy marks "per unit". "Despite their poor condition of health we can accept them as suitable." In another letter to the commandant it was stated that the experiments had been concluded, the women had died.

Certainly, during the war years, individual Christian doctors and scientists opposed euthanasia, but no physician in Germany, during the Nazi period, ever exposed the barbaric experiments on prisoners of war and other prisoners, to their students and colleagues, let alone protested against them.

My last days and weeks in Auschwitz have almost faded completely from my memory. The horror, the pressure, the undernourishment greatly diminished the ability of most of the prisoners to react. I remember how on one of the last days of October we marched naked past Mengele, who with a casual wave of his hand directed those whom he found fit for work to the right and the others to the left. Several times it happened that one of the emaciated figures whom he directed to the left, tried to go to the right side. Either he or his helper, an SS man as tall as he, grabbed the woman by the neck and threw her, over the heads of the other prisoners to the left side, where she remained lying on the ground.

About seventy French woman were chosen from our barracks to go on work assignment. The next day the usual disinfection was performed in a remote camp. Then each of them was issued a pair of pants, a dress and an overcoat or a jacket. My attire was a cotton dress and a grey, thin little summer coat.

Anni, on the other hand was lucky and got a splendid thick, black, long-haired winter overcoat. The dressing ceremony was concluded when other prisoners painted red crosses on our backs with some kind of oil paint.

Then we stood on the ramp for half a day and waited for the cattle cars to take us away. I don't know whether it was instinct or the need to have something to do while we were waiting for the cattle cars, but I kept scratching at the painted cross on Anni's back as she stood in front of me. The paint wasn't yet dry. I kept plucking and rubbing at the black wool hairs of her coat and the colored ends stuck to my hands and after only an hour, instead of a cross, only scattered dots of color could be seen on Anni's back. Suddenly Anni was standing in a normal, rather dingy winter coat among all the women marked with red.

This time the doors of the cattle car were opened wide during the trip. The cold wind blew through our mostly thin dresses. And yet, this transport seemed to me like a return to life. Past fields, villages and towns - there were houses, people, wagons, horses, cows and sheep; there were woods, hedges and trees. There was still a world of colors, without terrifying figures, without barbed wire, without watch towers.

Even the camp to which we were delivered three days later and which appeared to be a former mill, located on the edge of the Zittau mountains, did not seem so hopeless. There were no watch towers and the forested Sudeten mountains rose above us.

When we were led to the factory at five o'clock in the morning, or from the factory to the camp at six in the evening, we walked along a normal country road, past houses and gardens. We heard people talking and dogs barking.

As terrible as our situation was, hungry, worn out, filthy, freezing, I still no longer had the feeling that I was damned, banished, a living corpse in a realm of horror and shadows.

The camp was run by a constantly scolding, grey-uniformed policewoman. She was seconded by an SS man whose primary responsibility was the technical operation of the camp. Otherwise we were guarded once again by Gretchens, young women in uniform who had been drafted for this service; as one of them admitted to me, against their will.

When I described our fate to her, she had tears in her eyes, but assured me that she could do nothing, because she was strictly monitored by the camp commandant and the hardcore National Socialists. Thus it came about for example that when labor details were doing outdoor work and there was a hailstorm or snowfall, the most malicious Nazis among the female guards would take shelter with their group of prisoners, because they didn't want to get wet themselves. But the soft-hearted guards didn't dare stop working and we would be soaking wet and frozen when we returned to the camp.

There were about three hundred women in the camp: Hungarian, Dutch, French and some Polish women. We were here to work in a factory in Kratzau, a little town in the Sudeten district on the Neisse river, between Liberec (then called Reichenberg) and Zittau.

"If you work well, you get a bonus. Soap, for example, to wash yourselves with, or extra food. The workday is twelve hours with two twenty minute pauses so you can eat your bread."

"You get soup in the camp, mornings and evenings. Our guards, together with the foreman and his helpers, will watch you closely to make sure that you work well. If you can't work, you'll go back to Auschwitz and you know that the gas ovens there are waiting for you."

On the third day after our arrival we were taken to the factory. There was a day shift and a night shift. This meant that one bed was enough for two women. The one returning from the factory lay down on the bed which the other had left. The bed could even air out for a couple of hours. The kitchen staff, the room leaders and the prisoner Kapos and four or five Stubovas who cleaned the camp, were exempted from factory work. A Polish doctor was sent to work in the factory. Between four and five in the morning, before marching off to work, she was allowed to bandage a couple of wounds, disinfect boils, or give aspirin to a patient with fever.

None of the Dutch women had a steady job in the camp One or two of the French women were assigned to the kitchen. The room leader, a brutalized Hungarian, not a Jew, who had ended up in the camp because of some trouble over a man, had already been given a club. The other room leader had been chosen by the Nazis: Ursula Press, an eighteen year old German "half Aryan". She and her Jewish mother had been deported from Paris together with us. The mother, from Breslau, athletic and young-looking for her age, had survived all the selections, due to her resilient gait and her upright posture. She came from a very well-to-do manufacturer's family and had married one of her father's employees. In 1935 her husband had divorced her because due to his National Socialist convictions he did not want to live with a Jewish woman. However, he kept most of the family assets for himself.

She had immigrated to Paris with the daughter and part of the money. In 1941 her husband turned up in Paris where, as a big Nazi, he got an important job with the occupation authorities. In 1942 he took the daughter and employed her as a secretary and an intimate in his business dealings and his orgies. But after 1944 half-Jews also began to be arrested and he decided that his relationship with his daughter was too compromising. So he denounced both mother and daughter and they were arrested and taken to Drancy. Ursula, tall and blond, looked like the goddess Germania incarnate. She had taken on the crisp, cutting diction of the Nazis and soon became a favorite of the camp administration. Bellowing and swinging her club, she took charge of our room. Once again the satanic principle prevailed: prisoners were set to torment other prisoners to prevent solidarity from developing.

In the middle of November potatoes were brought into the camp. They had to be stored properly. Our food supply for the winter depended on keeping these potatoes safe, without losses. I volunteered for this work. I at least knew how to store potatoes. I and the others were busy unloading and uncovering and shoveling when the responsible SS boss appeared. He watched us awhile and suddenly said to me: "You shouldn't be working here; you should be in charge of the others and let them do the work." I said that the girls didn't know the work and I had to show them how to do it. Smiling ironically he looked me up and down and said in a rather paternal tone: "You with your knowledge, with your German culture and education, if you only wanted, you could have a totally different position here in the camp. You certainly would not have to work so hard."

As so often, I couldn't control my big mouth. "I'm not a German half-Aryan, so I'm not going to beat my comrades for a piece of bread."

For a moment I thought he was going to give me a beating, his face was so distorted with rage, but he just said through his teeth: "I'll see to it that you don't get out of here alive." He went out and after half an hour he sent Ursula, who told me, spitefully, that I should go get my soup at five that evening, because I was going on the night shift and had to leave with the others at five thirty.

The claim is made repeatedly that the population at large knew nothing about what was being done to the Jews. That might be true about events inside the death camps Auschwitz and Maidanek. But many people knew about the work details. Certainly we met only a few people when we were led through a village with our shaven heads, in rags and torn shoes, guarded by SS men and dogs. But in the factory we were seen by many people, in the work areas, in the corridors, or when we were shoveling coal. They could see that we were working twelve hour shifts without receiving any food or drink and that we worked in the snow and the rain without any head covering or stockings.

On one of the first days two German workers gave a couple of apples to two thin little French women. On the next day the female guards deliberately spread the news that the two workers had been taken away. In the camp we had no salt for our food and asked the Czech workers, who were working in the same hall as ourselves, to get us some salt. Three days later, when we started work in the morning, a little packet of salt was lying on one of our tables. None of the men dared to give it to us directly.

When the foreman or the guard wasn't looking, Anni succeeded in speaking with the Czechs. They knew about what was being done to us, but were extremely cautious. It was clear that they had been threatened.

The foreman, some of the skilled workers, some of the female apprentices and the management employees were Germans. I think a fourth of the work force were anti-Nazis who tried to help us. They were closely watched, so that only the most courageous and politically experienced of them succeeded in doing anything for us. Another fourth, the really confirmed Nazis, tried to add to our torments. But the remaining half of the employees behaved neutrally. They did nothing to harm us, but they gave us no help whatever. They simply looked away, happy to be in a safe situation. A probing question, a critical thought, could result in the questioner being sent to the front line.

There was a young girl working as an apprentice in our hall. A merry, dark-haired little Berliner, perhaps seventeen years old. When she tried to insert a work-piece into my automatic lathe, it didn't fit. "Yeah," I commented, "this piece of shit belongs on the junk pile. Careful or you'll squirt oil in your face." Astonished, she dropped the bar she was holding. "Where are you from? Why do you speak such good German? What are you doing here with the Polacks?" I explained that I was a born Berliner and that they weren't Polish, but French. "All you have to do is listen when they speak. In Paris they took us out of our apartments and away from our jobs and took everything away from us and shaved our heads and tattooed us," I showed her my arm, "and all the old people and children, who can't work, are killed."

She was totally aghast. It turned out that she and the other apprentices, who came from the most different German cities, had been told that these women were all Poles, who didn't want to work and had been brought here to teach them the work ethic. When I asked her, if these women were to be taught how to work, why did they have their heads shaved and why were they made to wear rags and why didn't they get warm food to eat, she seemed to become thoughtful. The next morning I saw her in a long conversation with the foreman. A bit later he walked by my machine, as if by accident and said: "You must not have enough to do, if you can tell all these big stories; you'd better worry about your machine!" From that morning on, the little Berliner stayed away from my workplace. A few days later, when she met me accidentally at the door, she said quickly: "I'm strictly forbidden to talk to you."

Despite the attempt to isolate us from all the other workers in the factory, the news that French and Dutch women were present spread like wildfire throughout the plant. Already on the second day two French forced laborers, so-called "free workers" came strolling through our hall with a cheery "bonjour, les Parisiennes" that worked like a ray of sunshine on a rainy day. From then on not a day passed without one of the Frenchmen finding something to do in the hall. A pat on the shoulder, accompanied by a "My little one. My brave one. My pretty one," cheered us up. We didn't feel quite so abandoned by the world. Even though they couldn't give us anything, they still brought us occasional news from the front and that was no small matter. A Frenchman slipped our Elisa a handmade map, that showed us for the first time where we were.

Once, while shoveling coal in the yard, we were working next to a group of Italian laborers. When they saw us they gave vent to their outrage. In Italian, French and German they cursed the barbarians and slave drivers. They instantly produced a couple of slices of bread, a couple of lumps of sugar, even some raisins and handed them to our girls. With effort I stuttered a question in Italian, asking about the political situation and where the Red Army was. This caused some excitement among the men. Suddenly a couple of clippings from Italian newspapers lay in front of my shovel. When I looked at them that evening, I learned that the Red Army was in Budapest.

I'll never forget the attitude of a small group of Soviet prisoners of war. It was on the day when we were putting the potatoes into storage. A group of Soviet prisoners was carrying out some sort of excavation project in the factory yard. While they were working, two soldiers with rifles stood nearby, but did not appear to take their guard duty very seriously. It was November 1944 and the treatment of Russian prisoners of war had already changed. These prisoners were not only wearing relatively clean and warm clothing, they did not appear to be starving. By this time, everyone knew that hundreds of thousands of German soldiers were prisoners in the Soviet Union. When the Red Army men saw us wretched French women, they stopped work and began to talk among themselves. Slowly one after the other pulled off whatever he could spare and threw it to the girls. Scarves, gloves, a knitted cap, even a little wool vest. The guards yelled a couple of times: "Get away from the girls. Verboten! Back to work!" – but by then it was all over.

I grasped the opportunity and walked slowly across the yard, close to the Soviet prisoners and mustering all my Russian I said "Good news, Soviet army in Budapest." All of them nodded happily to me, when I came back a little later, one of them made a sign. He smiled to me and pointed to a pile of bales of straw, some distance away. After the prisoners of war were gone, I dared to have a look. I don't think I ever again, in my whole life, got a gift that pleased me so much. Beneath the straw lay an enormous turnip and a shawl. A long, hand woven woolen shawl, grey, green and red.

Naturally I shared the turnip with Anni, Elisa and the others, but I only showed the shawl to Anni and kept it for myself. Anni immediately improvised a turban from it and put it on my head. Now my shorn head could no longer be seen. Anni also wore a hood. The skillful French woman had fashioned a hood attached to the coat, from the material of her coat, which was too long for her. The hood now completely hid the treacherous stubble on her head. My own bald skull had appeared, until now, to be the most important hindrance to our secret plans.

Since the first day, when we had been led in darkness down the three kilometer long road to the factory, we had thought about escape. Especially since we heard from the foreign workers that the advance of the Soviet army was temporarily halted, we had been discussing the possibility of escape. We were aware that the war was going to last out the winter.

Anni was becoming paler and thinner every day. Because she could not be treated in the camp, she bled from time to time. There was no doubt that she could stand this work and the lack of nourishment for one or two months more at most.

It was clear what would happen then. On the other hand, I was neither severely emaciated nor too weakened, but I suffered constantly from vitamin deficiency. I had the inflamed, bleeding gums, the cutaneous bleeding and above all the open infected wounds, that are symptomatic of scurvy. The condition had become catastrophic while I was working at the lathe and was not able to wash my oil-smeared hands and underarms with warm water and soap. After a few days my arms were covered with little boils. When the doctor disinfected a big pussy boil on my arm and bound it with a paper bandage, she wrinkled her brow and murmured the ominous word "phlegmon" (blood poisoning).

CHAPTER XII

1944

Escape from Auschwitz – A Thick Fog

"The fog formed a protective screen."

For Anni and me one thing was sure: we weren't going to survive this winter; no matter how slight our chances were, we wanted to take the risk.

It quickly became clear that our idea of finding our way to the Czech resistance movement was completely unrealistic. The few Czechs who had been allowed to remain in the Sudenten region were intimidated and almost as closely guarded as the forced laborers. On the other hand, we had the notion that we were in a Catholic area and could count on the aid of Christians. After all, in France I had experienced the solidarity of both German and French Catholics. Anni, who had lived in unoccupied France for a long time, also assumed that we could get help from Catholic priests.

Although I know of hundreds of cases from Italy, Belgium, France and Yugoslavia in which Jews found help and a hiding place in cloisters and churches, I have never heard of anything of the kind in the Sudenten area. According to everything I have been able to learn, in the Czechoslovakian Republic both German Catholics and German Protestants, from the very first day of the occupation by Hitler's army, cooperated completely with all the Nazi actions and supported them ardently. But at the time, fortunately, we didn't know that.

The first obstacle to our escape was our shaven skulls, which were completely bald. The tattoos on our arms were not a problem. Even in a short-sleeved dress they disappeared under the crust of dirt. The Red Cross from Auschwitz was still on my coat, but moisture and dust made it less visible. Because I could cover my head with the shawl, the gift of the Soviet prisoners of war, we now began to discuss seriously the possibility of an escape on the way to work. This march at five in the morning took place in total darkness. Even in the mountains all the blackout regulations were observed; once there had even been an air raid alarm at the factory. We marched in a column of fives and the four or five Gretchens who escorted us were supposed to maintain order among the thirty to forty ranks. That was a practical impossibility. We stumbled forward in the darkness, accompanied by constant cries of "Move it! Move it! Faster!" Sometimes a guard tried to shove a straggling prisoner back into line with a blow from her club, which caused even more confusion. Many of the prisoners had no proper shoes, which made them stumble and pull their neighbors down with them. Others could only walk with difficulty because of the wounds on their feet. In short, the two front ranks just behind the SS man who led the way with a lantern and the last rank, followed by an SS man with a storm lantern and a dog, were the only rows that could be effectively controlled, everything in between was a confused tangle.

And then, on November 1944, the unexpected happened. During our morning soup the camp commandant appeared with her deputy, the SS man and informed us that the labor force in the factory was to be reorganized.

We were going to work in new departments and at newly assigned places. The guards were going to assemble groups of twenty women each, who would then be distributed on arrival at the factory.

Anni pulled me over to a corner of the yard at once. "Teddy, it's now or never!"

"With this reorganization it will take a couple of hours before they find out that we're gone."

"There's always a big crush at the entrance of the tunnel and they can't keep track of everyone. We'll hide in the ditch there. When the SS man with the lantern and the dog is out of sight we'll meet in front of the tunnel entrance. We can't march with our French women. We'll line up with the Hungarians, they don't know us and when we're gone, all they will do is try to form a correct row of fives in front of the factory.

The tunnel was halfway up a slope, about a kilometer from the camp. A thick fog added to the darkness and no one noticed when I shoved my way out of line and squatted down in the ditch. After a few moments the SS man and his lantern disappeared in the tunnel.

I crept out of the ditch and looked for Anni, who couldn't be far off. Now the helpful fog became a problem. No silhouette, no form could be recognized, not a step could be heard, nothing. I tried stamping my feet, but the fog swallowed every sound. I crossed the road. Nobody. A cold shiver ran down my back. Did I dare call out? Should I go back? About fifty meters from the tunnel, I saw a shadow in the fog. I heard a faint call of "Teddy". Anni had also lived through a few minutes of terror.

At first we walked down the road in the opposite direction. We didn't know where it led, but we believed we were going to Liberec. When we noticed, fortunately, that we were not going to Liberec, we went in the other direction, to Zittau. The road, at this time, was completely empty and the fog formed a protective screen.

At about nine o'clock it started to get light and the morning haze was becoming more transparent, so that we glimpsed houses and a church tower in the valley. We decided to hide ourselves in the woods. We found some protection against the wind and the cold in a hollow with a flat bottom, where we covered ourselves as well as we could with fir branches. We tried without success to fasten a lapel of my coat with a fir needle, so as to hide the telltale red cross on my back.

I was worried. The soles of Anni's shoes were full of holes and walking was hard for her. Given her generally weakened condition, how long would it be before she succumbed to hunger, after our crusts of bread had been eaten? Anni, in her turn, felt my forehead and my pulse. A boil on my arm had swelled up so much that it could be seen through my dress and my hot forehead was not a good sign either.

Suddenly we heard dogs barking, shouts and whistles. We didn't dare to move. It sounded as if they had run the dogs up the mountain above us. More shouting and whistling and then we heard the barking from the road below. We both had the same thought, they're already hunting us with dogs, but we said nothing to each other. It got dark early, at about four in the afternoon. Now we could risk going down to the village. We were hoping to find a shed or a hay loft, in which we could be protected from the falling snow.

The village seemed deserted. Two or three children were running down a side street; a front door slammed shut ahead of us. Seeking refuge, we headed for the church. Our first big disillusionment: the church was shut. Was this a Protestant area? Or did they close the Catholic churches here in the evening? Next to the church stood a lovely big parsonage. A maid opened the door when we rang the bell; she looked at us critically but led us into the pastor's study.

A brightly lit room, oak furniture, a carpet. We were dazzled at first and could hardly recognize the portly grey-haired gentleman who was sitting in a chair behind a desk. Blue-eyed, red-cheeked, well nourished, in his velvet jacket he looked as though he had stepped out of a novel from the Romantic period of German literature. However, his expression was by no means friendly. Instead, he scrutinized our clothing and the puddles forming beneath our feet, with disapproval. "What do you want?" he asked severely.

I no longer know which one of us found the courage to explain quietly: "We are Jews and escaped from a camp. Can you help us?"

"How do you dare to come here!" he cried angrily. "I could be in danger myself! Leave the house at once! I want nothing to do with this. Get out of here, before I get into trouble!"

"Can we at least count on your discretion? You are a pastor, after all." Anni asked bitingly.

"Yes, yes, but get out!" With this he opened the door to the study and the front door and gave us an unmistakable nudge, so that we stumbled out into the dark street.

I don't know what I would have done if I had been alone. This scene first made me realize how desperate our situation truly was. Anni admitted later that at this moment she understood the foolhardiness and hopelessness of our flight. But because neither of us wanted to reveal her dejection to the other, we returned to the road and marched on along the valley. We tried to get into a hut and then a shed, but both had been locked up tight. It had become so dark, that we had a hard time recognizing the trees at the edge of the road. The fog swallowed up everything. But then we heard the noise of an approaching automobile. At this time of night that had to be the military or the police. As agreed, we jumped into the ditch and crouched beneath a pile of leaves.

The car stopped about a hundred meters from us. The dimmed spotlight only illuminated a narrow zone, about fifty centimeters above the ground. Men's voices sounded. High-topped military boots moved within the light cone. And the everything inside me became tense: two dogs, led on a leash. The command, "Search! Search!" could be understood. The dogs disappeared from our field of vision, the boots moved within the cone of light. Involuntarily our arms touched and we held hands with an iron grip. We didn't dare lift our heads. Again there was another command to the dogs. There was a short discussion, the boots disappeared and the car doors slammed – the car drove off.

The pastor had given the alarm that much was clear. We couldn't keep on walking along the road; instead we had to walk in the ditch or on the edge of the fields. Anni was dragging her feet more and more. Because her shoes were full of holes, she could feel all the rough spots, but neither of us wanted to admit our discouragement to the other.

Individual houses could be seen. They were situated on a riverbank and for good or bad we had to go across the bridge. Steps rang out on the bridge; two figures were coming towards us. In the fog we couldn't make out their clothing, but we could hear clearly that they were speaking French.

Anni tried to grab my arm to hold me back, but I had already run towards the two, gasping: "Are you French?"

"Of course," came the astonished answer and then I burst out: "Can you help us? We've escaped from a concentration camp. We don't have anything, no papers, no money, no decent clothes and they're probably looking for us."

"My God," one of them said. "We heard about a camp for French women and Dutchwomen about fifteen kilometers from here. We're prisoners and interned in a camp ourselves, but we go to work for a farmer every day. They don't have enough guards

anymore, so we go to work on our own. We can't take you into
the camp with us, but there's a hayloft at the farm and nobody
ever looks in there – it's awfully cold, though."

We felt such relief that we laughed at his misgivings. We decided
not to go through the village all together, but one of them would
lead one of us. Our helper, whose name was André, explained to
my escort which path he had to take to reach the farm. Then we
split up. We walked a good distance, talking about the camp and
the local situation and then he suddenly stopped:" What the hell,
I can't find the way, we should have been there by now."

For the third time that day my morale sank to zero, but I followed him without giving any indication of the way I felt. Then,
from a little side path, we heard "Psst, are you there?" and we
knew the others were waiting for us.

"No matter what happens, don't move around. Nobody ever
comes up here. I'll come sometime early in the morning. Good
night, my little ones." With these words André dispatched us up
the ladder into a hayloft, where we were able to build a service-
able burrow for ourselves, where we were concealed from anyone
looking up from below.

We lay there snuggled together in the hay and divided a big piece
of bread that André had given us at parting. My arm was hurting
badly, I was bathed in sweat from fever, but I still felt happy and
safe. André appeared the next morning. He was a lively, dark
blond young fellow with a face that inspired confidence. He came
from Avalon in Burgundy and reminded me a bit of the happy,
solid, wise Burgundian, whom Romain Rolland made immortal
in the character of Cola Breugnon. When André saw us in the
light of day, he was shocked. He found my appearance especially
alarming. I lay there apathetically, tormented by fever and it was
clear that for the next few days, there could be no talk of moving
on. André and Anni agreed on a plan. Besides the hot drink and
the bread that he had already brought us, we needed warm water

and soap so that we could at least wash our hands and face. And then, bandages and iodine, because in the night my abscess had burst and the pus had completely soaked through my sleeve. Also some piece of clothing without that compromising red cross on the back. In the barn André found an old worn-out coat belonging to the farmer. All I can remember is Anni pouring iodine on the abscess and applying a proper bandage, pouring a warm liquid into me and anxiously feeling my pulse. Later she admitted that she was by no means sure that I would leave the hayloft alive.

CHAPTER XIII

1944

Flight to Freedom

"My children are Nazis, they'll denounce you at once ."

André found a French forced laborer who was staying with civilians and who occasionally visited his comrades in the camp. At the train station, he bought two tickets to Dresden, a distance of ninety-five kilometers. In 1944 one needed a special permit to purchase a ticket for a trip of one hundred kilometers or more – a regulation that would later cause problems for us. The prisoners of war had collected the necessary money and there was eight marks left over; André handed this to us with a "bon voyage" and "merde". It was decided that we should take the night train to Dresden on Sunday. Hundreds of people would be traveling to Dresden to work at that time and we could board the train in the crush without attracting notice. Sunday was the fourth day after our escape and it seemed unlikely that the train stations would still be systematically watched. As we learned later from our Parisiennes from the camp, the search really had been abandoned on Sunday. Just as we had thought, due to the reorganization in the factory our absence was not noticed until some hours after the escape. At that point someone was sent to the camp. At the camp, a roll call was held and another was held at the factory, before it was finally discovered who was missing. When the SS chief at the camp learned that I was gone, he flew into a rage and ordered all the SS men to go out and search with dogs. But then it turned out that there was not a single thing in the camp that had belonged to us that could be given to the dogs to sniff. There wasn't even a bed.

Another woman was now sleeping on my straw sack. Nevertheless, the search party was out until late that night. On Sunday there was another roll call and a speech was made. We had been caught and now they were going to make an example out of us. "Their bread ration has been cancelled." The women, however, were not so stupid. If they had really caught us, then we would certainly have been brought back to camp and we would have been punished there as a warning to others. In fact, a Dutchwoman, influenced perhaps by our example, did attempt to escape later. She was caught and brought back to camp. Again there was a roll call and the unfortunate woman was tied to a stake and left there overnight. That was her exemplary punishment. By the next morning she had frozen to death.

In the overcrowded night train the tickets were not inspected. Soldiers, workers, farm women with bag and baggage sat and stood so tightly packed together that our clothing, fortunately, could not be seen in the dim light. Despite that, one man asked suspiciously where we were coming from, but our answer, that we were refugees from Upper Silesia who wanted to go to relatives in Dresden, seemed to satisfy him.

Suddenly Anni pushed me into a corner and whispered: "Teddy, don't move your head; if you do people will see the dirt on your neck." I tried to stand as rigidly erect as I could. The water and soap had only given me a cat's lick that reached only to the collar of my dress and the old jacket wasn't covering the dirt. Luckily Anni's neck was hidden by her hood.

Dresden, the Neustadt station, seven in the morning. People briskly coming and going: no one paid any attention to us. We tried the station restaurant, which was almost empty. How were we supposed to act here? What could we order without food ration coupons? How would the waitress react to our appearance?

Luckily self-service had been introduced and according to the menu only beverages could be purchased without a ration card.

There was also a telephone booth with a directory. I left the table to try and find the address of the Rehn coffee shop. Else Rehn, the wife of the owner, had once been my grandmother's pretty lady's maid. After her marriage, she and her husband had, with the financial aid of my grandparents, purchased a large bakery and café. When my father was in Dresden he always went there for the pastries, which were known throughout the city. Else had also visited us once or twice in Berlin. I found the address. But how great was my shock, when I came back from the telephone and saw that an army officer had taken a seat at our table. Tall, slender, impeccably attired, with a contemptuous expression on his face, he was staring inquisitively at Anni. Fortunately he was only able to see the relatively normal looking hooded coat; her torn shoes and naked legs were hidden from him. When I approached the table he immediately became wary and furrows appeared on his brow. He gave a hint of a bow and said in a brisk tone: "Excuse me, but do you know your way here in Dresden? I need to know how to get to Zellesch Way."

"No," I replied, avoiding any hint of a Berlin accent. "I'm sorry. We are complete strangers in this city. We've just arrived here. We come from Upper Silesia."

His demeanor changed at once. My perfect German had convinced him that we weren't foreign workers, or some kind of illegal foreigners on the prowl. He left the restaurant with a friendly greeting.

We arrived at the bakery shortly after eight. Although Else Rehn was certainly over fifty, she was still a beautiful woman. A child had just left the shop.

Nevertheless I spoke very quietly: "Good day, I am the grand-daughter of Consul General Schlesinger. I have escaped from a concentration camp. Can you help me?"

Else was so surprised that the only question that occurred to her was, which granddaughter I might be.

When I said "Lilli", she began to weep. "My God, little Lilli, who I liked so much. But I can't hide you here. You just don't know how things are. My children are Nazis, they'll denounce you at once and hand you over to the police. Sit down over there in the corner; I'll bring you something to eat."

Customers came to the shop. Else served them quickly. Then she brought us two cups of malt coffee and pastries and said, still with tears in her eyes, "I'm going to run up to my apartment and get some money. I'll put it in an envelope, which I'm going to place in front of the door in the corridor. When I'm back in the shop, you go out through the corridor and take the envelope."

And that's what happened. The envelope contained three hundred marks – a fortune at that time. But what could we buy without coupons? Could we purchase some kind of washing agent, perhaps a soap of the sort we had used in Paris? Were there still public baths?

At a drugstore we not only got soap paste, but for two marks we also purchased a bottle of liquid soap that smelled of disinfectant like an entire operating theatre. And quite nearby we found a public bath house with bath tubs. According to the price list, family cabins with two bath tubs were available. We climbed enthusiastically into the hot baths and used up half a bottle of our precious soap. The bandage on my arm loosened and pus from the abscess poured into the water. Anni was frightened, but all she could do was to pour soap on the abscess and then wipe off the arm and bind it up with toilet paper.

At this moment there was an energetic knock on the door. "When are you going to be done? You've been in there much too long already."

"Oh," Anni wailed, "we're refugees from Silesia. We spent the last three days in the train. We're so dirty that we can't get it all off with just one time."

"All right, but you're going to have to pay twice, understand?"

We were happy to pay after the second bath. Back on the street again, we felt somewhat more secure, despite our clothing.

Anni saw him first: a French soldier in uniform with a red cross armband was coming down the other side of the street, in no particular hurry. "A first aid man," she whispered. But I had already run across the road and spoke to him openly: "Can you help us? We've escaped from a camp. We don't have papers and we need shelter."

He looked searchingly at Anni and me. "That's hard. I'm a prisoner of war myself. We can't shelter anyone and the free laborers can't do that either. But there is a French woman from Alsace living in Neustadt, who is married to a German tavern keeper. She has helped her compatriots quite often. Maybe she can put you up for a couple of nights without papers. But be careful, everyone here mistrusts the French." He gave us the address and explained what streetcar we had to take.

It was already getting dark. when we entered the small smoky tavern. The tall, portly, red-cheeked tavern keeper was at his post behind the bar. With his crew cut, his little pig eyes and his bloated, expressionless face, he looked like something from the film version of an operetta. We asked for his wife.

His wife wasn't at home and wouldn't be back anytime soon, he said bad-temperedly and looked at us full of mistrust. What did we want with her anyway? Anni and I exchanged glances. "Oh, we just wanted to say hello." We bought lemonade, drank it quickly and left.

Now Kipsdorf was our only remaining possibility. In the train to Dippoldiswalde I explained the situation to Anni. As a child I was constantly ill with cold-related ailments and I was frequently sent, both in summer and winter, to recover at a children's' home at Kipsdorf in the Erz Mountains. The home was run by the four unmarried Hoffmann sisters. Two of them had trained as nurses with the Lutheran deaconesses and they were not only militant Protestants, but German Nationalists and loyal to the Kaiser. Everything indicated that these ladies would consider Hitler much too plebian and the Nazi ideology much too un-Christian.

We got to the Kipsdorf station at about nine at night. Despite the darkness, I found the way to the Klara Maria House. When we rang, a young girl answered the door and explained that the Hoffmann ladies were not available at such a late hour; they had already retired to their rooms. If we would tell her what we wanted, she was authorized to deal with any requests.

"I'm sorry to disturb the ladies, but this is a very private matter that really has nothing to do with the children's' home. Couldn't you be so kind and call one of the sisters?"

Shaking her head, she let us come into the vestibule, went upstairs and reported on the two women waiting below and their request. "What sort of women are they," asked Miss Berta, the youngest of the sisters," educated women or simple women from the village?" After a moment's reflection the girl answered: "Well, sort of half-educated."

Miss Berta now entered the vestibule and regarded us with astonishment and suspicion. I told her my name and where I was coming from. She did not doubt for a moment the facts of our escape from the "Jew camp". "Lilli Schlesinger," she cried, "always the best student in the Sunday School class." In this regard her memory was better than mine. "Come upstairs!"

And then we were in the brightly lit, elegant Biedermeier parlor of the Misses Hoffmann, sitting at a table covered with a snowy white damask cloth and a silver tea service. We hardly dared touch the sandwiches. We felt as if we had landed on another planet and we both hesitated to bring all the horror of our existence into this peaceful room. Still, it was necessary to tell the truth to our helpers. They were not totally unprepared. "Nothing these barbarians do could surprise us. And now the German nation has to pay for what it has done to other people. That is the punishment."

The only thing I found shocking was that even these honest, helpful and courageous Christian women still made distinctions among human beings. When I spoke very cautiously about the fact that Jews and Gypsies, the elderly, children and pregnant women had been gassed and burned, I got the answer: "We believe everything you say and we know what the Nazis are capable of. After all, they have even killed incurably ill German adults and abnormal German children."

The sisters knew precisely the danger to which they were exposing themselves by helping us. My abscess was treated, our rags were burned and the clothing we received was respectable, tidy, warm and inconspicuous. The only thing I kept was the shawl that the Soviet soldiers had given me.

We decided to travel to Lake Constance and to cross the border illegally into Switzerland, in an area that I was well acquainted with. The sisters looked up the train route in the railway guide: Chemnitz, Plauen, Bayreuth, Nuremberg, Crailsheim, Stuttgart, Radolfzell. We were instructed how to behave in the train. During an air raid we had to look for the nearest cellar at once. We should say that we were refugees who had lost everything, including our papers.

The first day of the journey passed uneventfully. The trains were filled with weary travelers. It was easy to obtain tickets at the various train stations. We appeared to be normally dressed. Other refugees also looked pale and emaciated. People simply regarded us as two women who had been through a lot. Nobody asked us any questions. A soldier, certainly no younger than I was, offered me his seat, tapped me on the shoulder and said affably, "Have a seat, Mama!"

As long as our train was passing through Saxony and the Vogtland, our fellow travelers still, somehow, believed in Hitler: fearmongers were not allowed. Hitler's going to teach the English and the Russians a lesson! He's going to wipe them off the map. The new weapons – they'd better be scared. Just hold out and see it through. These foreign workers, these lazy bums, they need to learn how to work!

That changed after we crossed the border into Bavaria. The further the train traveled towards the southwest, the fuller it became. Soldiers, refugees carrying nothing but little handbags, young girls and women who had been drafted into service and were underway to some duty station, old people from the coast, looking for shelter in Bavaria. Now we began to hear from soldiers and civilians: there's no point anymore! My God, when will it end. How much longer is it supposed to last?

Will I ever see my home again? There was so much complaining and name-calling that we got scared. What would happen if the military police or a Gestapo man were to check the entire car, in order to arrest the agitators? We would be trapped. The police would never believe that we were refugees who had lost our papers. But it looked as if political surveillance was no longer functioning so well in Bavaria.

Unmolested, we left the train in Nuremberg and bought a ticket for Crailsheim, for a train that was supposed to leave at midnight. We were just looking for the right platform, when the sirens sounded. Air raid. How should we behave? Where was the nearest air raid shelter? Would papers be checked there? Were some shelters for civilians and others for soldiers? We decided to join a group of men and women who were crowding and shoving each other in the corridors, so that we were able to mingle with them. In their midst we hurried down a flight of stairs and found ourselves in a cellar where respectably attired burghers sat, suitcase in hand, next to tired soldiers and shabbily dressed elders and women who were guarding their sacks and straw suitcases with an air of mistrust. We even managed to secure a place on a bench and waited for the all clear in a fairly relaxed frame of mind.

When the sirens sounded again, we had gained a new experience. Once again we followed the stream of humanity: it ended in the waiting room. The hall was full of travelers, all facing many hours of waiting. We bought ourselves an unidentifiable warm drink and sat down at a table where three elderly soldiers were already sitting. Three hours till train time. Dead tired, we laid our heads on the table and fell asleep at once. "Your papers, please!"

Frightened, we sat up straight. Two military policemen were standing at our table. The soldiers handed over their papers, which were checked very carefully. We sat there, motionless. The military police paid no attention to us, saluted and left. They were only checking military papers. Reassured, I let my head droop and immediately went back to sleep. A sharp shove woke me. "Teddy, we have to go, otherwise we'll miss our train." It was Anni's voice. I looked at the clock. "Don't we have time?"

"Come on!" that sounded so urgent that I stood up, sighing.

In the main hall of the station Anni explained: The two military policemen were only checking the soldiers, but at the far end of the waiting room she had seen two uniformed police, who were only checking civilians.

Our train was due to leave in one and a half hours. We couldn't stay in the empty main hall, that was too conspicuous. And travelers were only on the platforms when a train was about to arrive. The only place where we did not have to fear the police was the toilet. We went there.

We loitered there, began washing ourselves and explained to the woman attendant that we had been traveling for three days. The woman was sympathetic and not averse to having a chat with us. And now we were helped by the good advice of the Hoffmann sisters. Anni had to take off her hood in order to wash her face and neck and the stubble on her head could be seen. "Oh," she said quickly, "isn't that terrible, when Stettin was bombed, all my beautiful long hair was singed; it got all yellow and stinking and I had to get it all cut off." Bombing and fire – those were the key words. In the last hour before our train left, we learned how many times the main station at Nuremberg had been bombed and why the Bavarians were so tired of the war. How pessimistic Nuremberg had become, that city once devoted to Hitler! How many cities in southern Germany had been rendered almost uninhabitable?

As we sat in the train, we thought we had learned how to behave during an air raid. But we soon learned otherwise. In Bad Cannstatt, shortly before Stuttgart, the one hundred kilometer limit had once again been reached. We had to get out and buy the next ticket. But, oh horror, the exit was closed. A siren sounded. It's a warning signal, two men said and invited us to board the Stuttgart train, otherwise we would be stuck here. And so we followed the other passengers, who were going to a train on the track across from us. At the next station we got out with the others. Unsuspectingly I gave our tickets to the girl at the barrier. "Just a moment. You've gone past the limit," the ticket inspector said severely.

"Yes, we couldn't get off the platform in Cannstatt, so we just rode further."

"But you know that's a violation." This time her tone was still more severe.

"There was an air raid warning," said a man behind us.

"That doesn't matter, the rules are the rules. We're here to enforce them."

"But then, what should I do?" I asked, trembling. Now they were certainly going to demand our papers.

"Then you will just have to pay five marks fine each," came the menacing reply.

In the train to Radolfzell, our last stop before the border, we laughed about the ten marks that had saved our lives. But already there were new problems. We had to continue on foot. Looking downstream, the right bank of this arm of Lake Constance, the Untersee, was German and the left bank was Swiss, but at Stein on the Rhine, where the river leaves the lake, there is a Swiss enclave on German soil. The little Swiss town lies on both sides of the Rhine and Swiss territory extends along the right bank for a few kilometers up to the wooded heights. I knew the area quite well from my time at the boarding school in Gaienhofen, but I still hadn't been to Lake Constance in more than ten years. It was already getting dark. In Radolfzell I couldn't find the street leading down to the Untersee. A person we asked showed us the way, but added that it was a closed area and that we couldn't enter it without a special permit.

I don't know where we got the courage, but we simply kept on marching down the country road and after an hour I began to recognize the landscape again. The dark surface of the lake appeared on our left. A cold wind was blowing from that direction and a billowing fog crept slowly up to the roadway. To our right, the forest began to ascend. We walked on. When we rounded the next curve our doubts disappeared: over there, perhaps two kilometers off, lights twinkled across the lake. In Steckborn, that little Swiss town, houses and streets were lit up bright to send us a signal: this is neutral Switzerland! It was like a fairytale, the lights of the magic castle and the country of the good fairies. A town with shining lights! The sight gave us new courage and spontaneously we began to walk faster.

"Halt! Stop right there! What are you doing here?" Two shapes approached us. In the darkness we saw the outlines of two men in uniform, one of them leading a dog on a leash.

As always in a critical situation, Anni reacted with the speed of light: "Oh my, you scared us just now," she said in the affected voice of a frightened maiden. "I thought you were two bandits coming out of the forest!"

"And what would you have done, all alone in the dark, if it really had been bandits?" One of the soldiers picked up her tone at once.

"Oh God," Anni squeaked, "then we would have run away and called for help and then you would have come."

Pleased, they both laughed and inquired where we were going so late in the evening. "To Gaienhofen Castle," I said deliberately, knowing that only local people called the country school "the Castle".

"You live there, or work there?"

"No, we want to go to my aunt, Dr. Haldimann. We come from Freiburg and we were bombed out and lost our apartment and everything we owned."

That made an impression. They spoke a few well-intended words, cracked a few jokes with us and warned us to be careful. And then they and the dog went on without further questions.

We took to heart the warning to be careful. We left the road to look for a path through the hills. The lake and the lights of the town reflected in it were like a guidepost pointing the way to the Promised Land.

We rested in the woods. Anni's feet were raw from walking. We heard a dog barking, not very far off. We had to move on, as quickly as possible. Abruptly, the path stopped. In front of us lay an orchard, surrounded by barbed wire. It wasn't so hard to crawl through. We kept moving westward through the trees; then barbed wire again and then sure enough, there was our path again, on the far side of the wire, leading across the hills to the border. This time, though, the wires were strung very taut, leaving no spaces. We could climb up the posts and mount over the fence that way. I was able to do it without a lot of difficulty.

There was a stone on the other side and I stood on it to give Anni a hand. She was very weak and her condition worried me. With one hand on the post and holding tight to me with the other, she wanted to slide over the fence. But we hadn't taken account of her thick, heavy coat. The hem of the coat got hooked on the barbed wire when Anni fell across the fence. She hung head down on the fence, unable to speak. With her hands on my shoulders she tried to brace herself and pull free from the wire. All in vain: the coat held fast. Would this be our end, so close to the goal? I began pulling and tearing at the coat with all the strength I had left. It seemed to be made of iron. Anni also kept trying to free herself somehow, but our combined strength wasn't enough. Filled with desperation, I yanked and tore. Suddenly there was a thump and Anni was lying on the ground. She tried moving her arms and legs; everything seemed to be working and after a couple of minutes she had recovered from her shock enough to stand up and start moving, painfully.

Meanwhile, the fog that had helped us so much had thickened, but when we came out of the woods and the path began to go downhill, we saw a shimmer of light in the valley below. That had to be Stein on the Rhine. Directly below us we saw a couple of houses, which were lighted.

"Anni, you can rest now. Do you see those houses lit up down there? That means we're in Switzerland."

But cautious Anni was not to be placated so easily. "I'm not so sure about that. It can't be that simple. I think the last farm houses in Germany might switch on a few lights, just to profit from Swiss neutrality."

Slowly and carefully we went on our way. Again the path was interrupted, this time by a trench, bordered on the far side by another barbed wire fence, which we climbed over without trouble. Now we were in a vineyard.

"And what's that up there?," Anni whispered, "that looks like a watch tower." In fact, we could see the outlines of a long building, shimmering through the woods.

"Oh, you're seeing ghosts. That's a hay barn, come on." I took her by the hand and bending over we crossed through the vineyard and climbed over another barbed wire fence and across another trench. We were on the road to Stein. Barely a hundred meters down the road a man in uniform came out of the fog.

"Are you Swiss or German?" we asked without beating around the bush.

"I'm Swiss, can't you see that?"

As if by command we both began to sob; we flung ourselves at him, threw our arms around him and squeezed his hand.

Slowly and thoughtfully he looked us over from head to foot. "Yes, well now, where did you come from?"

"Over there, through the vineyard, through the trenches."

"That's impossible. Do you know that you marched right by that German border station – a stone's throw away?"

CHAPTER XIV

Return to Life – Michael

". . . the first sign of life that Jascha had from me in thirteen months."

We reached the neutral soil of Switzerland on December 3, 1944. The first reaction of the Swiss customs officer was one of hesitation. He doubted whether we would be recognized as refugees. But after seeing our tattooed prison numbers and our shaven heads, he declared sympathetically that, while there could be no more doubt about our status, he must, unfortunately, hand us over to the police. At the prison in Schaffhausen, the police were very kind and helpful. We stayed there only two days and then were sent on to Basel. In Basel we were taken to a military camp, where the regimen was "strict but fair". After three weeks of quarantine I asked the commandant to allow me to get in touch with the French consul, so that I could get word to my husband. He replied that I should be happy to have saved my life and not go making difficulties for him. Eight days later we were transferred to another military camp in Montreux on Lake Geneva. We were still behind barbed wire and guarded by the Swiss, but the francophone officers and soldiers showed more understanding for our situation.

I finally succeeded in smuggling a message out of the camp and into France. It was the first sign of life that Jascha had from me in thirteen months. When Jascha's answer reached me at the beginning of February 1945, we were in our third military camp in Ricon in Doestal, a town that even my Swiss friends had not heard of before. The message was that Jascha too had survived everything. During a street raid, a few months before the liberation of Paris, he simply ran from the police. After the liberation he was able to return to his laboratory and now he resumed his scientific work.

Our son André had been hidden and since the liberation he had been in the care of a private nurse. Although he was still in a full body cast, the doctors were, at this time, more optimistic. Jascha informed me that our Bavarian friend and helper, Max Gall, had escaped to Switzerland with his French wife and children when the German army wanted to mobilize him in June 1944. After everything he had done for us during the German occupation, I was now able to turn to him once again for help. And in fact after a few days Max Gall was able to get us transferred to a refugee hostel at Neuhaus near Schaffhausen. Here we not only got shelter and food, we were even paid a little pocket money for the simple sewing tasks that we performed and were allowed to move freely within a fifteen kilometer radius. Meanwhile Professor Pieron, together with other French scientists, put all the wheels in motion to make it possible for Anni and me to return to France. The war had not yet ended when we returned to Paris on March 25, 1945.

In May 1945 I learned that I was pregnant. Unfortunately my health had been severely damaged and I had not yet recovered. When our son Michael was born, on December 27, 1945, just nine months after my return, the doctors determined that his bone structure was more than fragile. He was a sickly child, who needed special care for years. He was seven years old before he exhibited physical development commensurate with his age. We didn't have our own apartment then and our friend Franka let us have a big room in hers. It wasn't until 1947 that we succeeded in renting two furnished rooms with a kitchen in the Rue des

Lilli's sons André and Michael

Lilli's sons André and Michael
with father Jascha

Martyrs directly on the Place Pigalle. We had to pay a premium, on top of the rent. The apartment was infested with bedbugs and we had to keep the light on all day long, but at least we could live together as a family. We got along well with the "ladies" of the Place Pigalle, some of whom lived in our building.

André was once again our problem child. A recurrence of his spinal-cord tuberculosis forced us to put him back in a full body cast and to place him in a sanatorium in Switzerland. Our meager salary as scientists didn't enable us to pay all the costs arising from his treatment. We tried constantly to cover our expenses from translations, preparing documents, articles and working for a film company.

In the fall of 1945 Jascha was named Charge de Recherche at the Collège de France. I found a position in a documentation center which belonged to the Ministry of Agriculture and where work was also performed for the United

Nations Educational Scientific and Cultural Organization, as well as for the Food and Agricultural Organization. I took correspondence courses and passed my examination as a scientific documentarian. Together with young French comrades we made propaganda for the Soviet sciences and participated in every political action at our workplace. My boss, a very conservative Frenchman, reproached my bourgeois and rather anti-Communist colleagues for making common cause with me in matters relating to working conditions and pay. But for the most part our political disputes, in which Jascha also occasionally joined, were a source of intellectual pleasure for him. He offered us his help in case we wanted to become naturalized French citizens and expressed bafflement when we declined and explained that we were completely satisfied with our Soviet citizenship.

In 1948 our Lithuanian passports with the consular stamp were transformed into Soviet passports for use outside the USSR. When he gave us the passports, the consul admonished us to refrain from all political activity in France. He even criticized our membership in the union. But we refused to resign from the union because our French colleagues were counting on our support. We withdrew from all work for the Communist Party and fortunately our reputations as resistance fighters and anti-Fascists were so good that our friends and fellow workers did not hold it against us. In autumn 1952 we were summoned again to the Soviet consulate. The consul suggested that we resettle in the German Democratic Republic. And so it came about that at Christmastime of that year we flew to Berlin with André, age eleven and Michael, seven. Jascha founded the Institute for General Biology and organized the first courses in radiation biology and biophysics. During our first years in Berlin I worked as a free lance translator and document expert. At that time there were still very few trained French interpreters, thus my services were in constant demand. But I wanted to return to science and to work with Jascha, so I took my degree in biology at the Agricultural Institute in Berlin and became an assistant in Jascha's institute.

Lilli and Jascha working together

We have found our true home here in the GDR (German Democratic Republic, also known as East Germany).

CHAPTER XV

POST SCRIPT TO THE 1991 EDITION

O n the basis of his scientific publications, Jascha was called to a professorship at the Humboldt University. There he founded the Institute for General Biology, where students were trained beginning in 1954. At the end of the 1950s he organized the first courses in radiation biology and biophysics, before a special institute for the study of these subjects had been founded.

During the first years of our residence in the GDR I worked as a free lance document expert and translator. Because there were, at that time, very few French translators, I was constantly called upon by academies, ministries and trade unions to act as interpreter for important delegations or at congresses. Although I enjoyed traveling to Geneva, Helsinki, North Africa and even China, the constant separation from my children and husband became too much for me and I wanted to return to scientific work.

At the end of 1956 I began working at the Institute for General Biology under the supervision of my husband. In 1959 I received my doctorate from the Agricultural Faculty in Berlin. My dissertation was in the field of plant physiology.

In the meantime I had completed a course of study in immunology and during the following years I worked in this field as my husband's chief assistant. Although there were a number of difficulties during these years, the work with a number of assistants and students was still satisfactory. Today former colleagues and students still come to us with problems and they tell us that they retain good memories of the time they spent at the institute, both for professional reasons and in terms of human relations.

During the years 1967-1975 my husband was invited for long periods of time to Cuba and Mexico as a guest lecturer. He also organized postgraduate courses for physicians, veterinarians and biologists. I assisted him in teaching the practical courses.

We have been active together for 36 years and look back on this time with positive feelings. It has always been of great importance to us to educate young people in the spirit of humanism, progress and friendship among nations.

Lilli and Jascha reunited